"Albert Einstein said, "Try not to become a man of success, but rather a man of value. Over the course of my life, I have read thousands of books designed to inform, entertain, and persuade. A rare few were impactful, even transformational. ***On Mission with Purpose*** *by Steven Garofalo is such a book.*

Drawing wisdom from the most transformational book in history, the Bible, along with insights from ancient philosophers and leaders as well as modern-day cultural influencers, Steven addresses some of the most pressing and fundamental questions that have challenged mankind through the ages: Why am I here? How can I find meaning and purpose in life? What does true success look like for me? Will my life have any significance beyond my lifetime?

Like many young men of my generation, I struggled to find the connections between purpose, meaning, mission, and success. I was told by my elders to simply work harder and success would follow. As a result, I struggled for years to find my personal and my professional identity.

Having just celebrated my seventy-third birthday, ***On Mission with Purpose*** *challenged my assumptions about retirement and encouraged me to reconsider my future plans so I can continue to make a difference in the lives of others and finish well."*

Arch N. McIntosh, Jr.
Headmaster Emeritus
Charlotte Latin School

"In a world of confusion and uncertainty, Steven Garofalo, in his new book ***On Mission with Purpose*** *cuts through all the noise and competing voices to show clearly how to live a life of purpose, meaning, and mission and leave a lasting legacy for generations to come. At one time or another, we all have asked, "Why was I born? What is my purpose here on earth?" Steven provides timeless wisdom in answering these important questions and helping each of us to figure out our life purpose and mission. He gives practical ways that we can fulfill our God-given mission in the short time we have here on earth. Take the journey*

with Steven to find out your individual God-given purpose and mission to live a fulfilled life and leave a lasting legacy."

Michael Keating
Chief Financial Officer
Park Rug Company, Inc.

"Having been in ministry over forty-five years, it's refreshing to read such an amazingly practical book. This is a solid, encouraging entry in the Christian purpose/leadership genre. Steven Garofalo avoids fluffy name-it-claim-it vibes and instead roots everything in Scripture, real-life messiness (his burnout, family stories, business examples), and evidence-based insights (purpose literally correlates with better health, longevity, and immune function—studies back this up). The Trifecta framework is simple yet powerful: Purpose without mission is like owning a fully loaded Tesla that you never drive!"

Dr. Wilson Morales
Lead Pastor
Encounter Christian Center
Charlotte Hall, MD

*"**On Mission with Purpose** by Steve Garofalo is a must-read for all mature believers, especially those engaged in any form of ministry within their local church.*

I was particularly drawn to chapter three, "The Necessity of Resistance." I strongly resonate with Garofalo's conviction that "resistance is necessary to make you strong—physically, mentally, and spiritually." In my own book on leadership development, I describe a season of life that comes to us all—a season of conflict. I emphasize that trials and difficult times are inevitable; none of us can escape them. They are part of God's process in shaping His chosen vessels.

Through interviewing 368 leaders across six nations, I discovered that these "dark nights of the soul" are universal. They come to believers and unbelievers alike. However, in Christ, we as believers are given the grace and strength to endure and overcome.

In my current season of life—having crossed the threshold of my sixties—I deeply connected with chapters 12, 13, and 14. As I embrace a season of legacy and succession, passing the baton of leadership to my daughters and sons-in-law, every word served as both encouragement and inspiration to remain faithful, stay the course, and finish well.

I wholeheartedly recommend this book."

Dr. Eddie J. Fernandes, DMin

Founder of Riverside International Church, Portugal

Author of *From Chaos to Christ-Likeness, Jesus the Jew I Never Knew, Women in Leadership, The 12 P's of Biblical Masculinity*

*"**On Mission with Purpose** argues that true fulfillment comes from aligning your life with a deeper purpose rooted in a biblical foundation and a life of following Jesus, rather than chasing success, money, or status. Garofalo frames life as a progression from purpose to meaning to mission, where purpose is the foundation, meaning gives you the "why," and mission is where the rubber meets the road. He emphasizes that adversity and resistance are essential in refining character, strengthening faith, and clarifying direction, while challenging modern definitions of success and pointing instead to a life aligned with God's will through service, discipline, and lasting significance.*

The call of Jesus on our lives is to live with purpose and walk that out with Him and others. This book gives practical direction on how to do that. It is a strong, faith-driven message that cuts through the noise and provides a practical road map for living it out. This book is a wake-up call. It helps you get back on track with what matters most in your life with Jesus and others.

Thanks again, Steven, for inviting me to endorse this book. A genuine honor. A great time of reflection and a little kick in the butt for me as I prayerfully consider our next steps in ministry too."

Dan Cotter, VP, Finance & Operations

Cigar Association of America, Inc. Pipe Tobacco Council, Inc.

"In a culture that prizes platform and clout, Steven Garofalo reminds us of an approach to life that is quieter but more substantial. An approach that is not seeking attention but seeking depth and authenticity—first with God and then with others. Steven (or "Stevie G." as I tend to call him) is a close friend. Closeness brings proximity and proximity the opportunity for scrutiny. His views on success, purpose, and mission are worthy of consideration because he lives them. I recommend ***On Mission with Purpose*** *to the reader for thoughtful reflection and practical integration of purpose to mission into one's life."*

J.T. Bridges, PhD
Professor of Philosophy
Southern Evangelical Seminary

"This book provides a clear and encouraging guide to living with purpose, blending testimony, Scripture, and practical advice. It's a meaningful read for anyone wanting a faith-centered take on mission and legacy."

James A. Littlejohn, MBA, MS
Financial Services Executive

"We live in a culture where young people are desperately searching for identity and meaning to life—often in all the wrong places. Steven Garafalo has structured a book that weaves its way through an entire lifetime as it addresses mission and purpose. First, he points to the true basis of where to find identity, Jesus Christ. The road map continues through the value of finding meaning in work—even the necessity of resistance—to the value of finishing the race well. With insights relevant to every stage of life, this book speaks to people of all ages and vocations seeking to live with purpose, always returning to the central question, "Whom do you serve?"

Lisa Littler

*"Due to my military background, I don't have much room for fluff in my life, employing tools that are functional and effective. So, in a distinct military term, here is the BLUF (Bottom Line Up Front). Steven's latest book, **On Mission with Purpose**, is a transformational guide for readers seeking to discover their true God-given purpose that gives their life meaningful value, while developing insight to walk their path to embrace the mission. This book challenges readers to recalibrate their priorities, embrace resistance as a tool for growth, and build a legacy that transcends time, utilizing thought-provoking reflections and actionable advice with clarity and directional focus. It is a must-read for Christians/for anyone desiring to live a life of significance and leave a lasting impact on the world they encounter."*

Don Dodson
Speaker, Teacher
MA Christian Ministries, Homiletics and MA Management and Leadership
CW5 (Ret.) Corporate Pilot

*"Almost thirty years ago, my youth pastor asked a question that sticks with me even today, "What are you going to do with your dash?" He then showed us a picture of tombstone with the birth and the death date. The dash in between the dates was highlighted. Steven Garafalo's new book is an important guide to helping us all not only find out what our dash is but also what steps we must take to live out this dash. Knowing our true purpose and living into it is a satisfaction and reward far beyond anything this world offers. Whether you are a young schoolteacher or an executive on the cusp of retirement, this book has a message for you. It is never too early or too late to begin to understand and find out how we all must be **On Mission with Purpose**."*

Scott Elliott, Pastor for Families and Youth
Spirit of Joy Lutheran Church, Weddington, NC

STEVEN GAROFALO

ON MISSION WITH PURPOSE

Maximize Your Potential by Living a Life of Meaning

Charlotte, NC

On Mission with Purpose
Copyright 2026 Steven Garofalo
Published by TriedStone Publishing Company
3122 Fincher Farm Rd., Ste. 100-216
Matthews, NC 28105
www.TriedStonePublishing.com

Editor: Denise Loock

Cover design: John Brandenburg

Printed in the United States of America

Library of Congress Cataloging-in-Publication Data
Library of Congress Control Number: 2026942670
Garofalo, Steven
On Mission with Purpose / Steven Garofalo

ISBN 978-0-9897446-8-3 (TPB: Alk. Paper)

1. Apologetics. 1. Garofalo, Steven. (Steven Garofalo),

LLCN 2026942670

To Mom

Your name, Vita, (Italian for life) says it all regarding living with mission, purpose, and meaning.

Some lessons are taught, while others are caught. We four kids caught your life example as the model for living out our lives with great love, selflessness, purpose, meaning, and mission. Had you not done so, I would not have been able to write this book. You always give credit to God, telling me, "Steven it was by the hand of God that you were able to do this.

On behalf of John, Gary, Gail, and myself, we adore, respect, appreciate, and love you deeply, well beyond what words can express.

Mission accomplished, Mom.
I dedicate this book to you.

Love,
Your son Steven

I have fought the good fight, I have finished the race, I have kept the faith. Henceforth there is laid up for me the crown of righteousness, which the Lord, the righteous judge, will award to me on that day, and not only to me but also to all who have loved his appearing.

2 Timothy 4:7–8 (ESV)

Well done, good and faithful servant. You have been faithful over a little; I will set you over much. Enter into the joy of your master.

Matthew 25:21 (ESV)

Behold, what I have seen to be good and fitting is to eat and drink and find enjoyment in all the toil with which one toils under the sun the few days of his life that God has given him, for this is his lot. Everyone also to whom God has given wealth and possessions and power to enjoy them, and to accept his lot and rejoice in his toil—this is the gift of God. For he will not much remember the days of his life because God keeps him occupied with joy in his heart.

Ecclesiastes 5:18–20 ESV – King Solomon, ca. 935 BC

So I decided there is nothing better than to enjoy food and drink and to find satisfaction in work. Then I realized that these pleasures are from the hand of God. For who can eat or enjoy anything apart from him? God gives wisdom, knowledge, and joy to those who please him. But if a sinner becomes wealthy, God takes the wealth away and gives it to those who please him. This, too, is meaningless—like chasing the wind.

Ecclesiastes 2:24–26 NLT – King Solomon, ca. 935 BC

TABLE OF CONTENTS

The two most important days in life
are the day you are born
and the day you find out why.

Attributed to Mark Twain

FOREWORD

There are moments in life when the world seems to slow just enough for us to reflect on the journey we have traveled and the road that lies ahead. In these moments, we ask ourselves the most profound questions: Why am I here? What truly matters? Am I living my days with intention, or am I simply reacting to the demands of the world around me? Over many years of leadership and personal growth, I have wrestled with these questions myself. The answers have shaped not only my career but also the legacy I hope to leave behind. That is why I am greatly honored to introduce Steven Garofalo's new book, ***On Mission with Purpose***. This book will guide leaders who yearn not just for success but also for a life of significance.

I have known Steven Garofalo personally for many years, and he lives a life of purpose. Steven is the ideal person to have published this book.

This book could not be timelier. We are living in an era of unprecedented change, with shifting social norms, technological advances, and global challenges that demand both resilience and resolve. In such an environment, leaders are called to more than operational excellence—they are called to live and lead with purpose. Purpose is not a destination; it is a journey, one that requires courage, reflection, and a willingness to embrace both the triumphs and the trials along the way. Purpose is being obedient to God. Jeremiah 29:11 makes this fact clear: "*For I know the plans I have for you,*" declares the Lord, "*plans to prosper you and not to harm you, plans to give you hope and a future*" (NIV).

Early in my journey, in my mid-twenties and early thirties, I grappled with the concept of purpose. I was an unbeliever at the time, after graduating from the Ivy League Cornell University with a PhD in biochemistry in 1983, when the biotech industry was exploding. I was driven, ambitious, and even hyper-ambitious. I was eager to make an impact, but I often found myself feeling unfulfilled despite outward achievements. It wasn't until I began to intentionally explore what truly motivated me—honoring God in all that I do, including the core values and beliefs that formed the foundation of my life—that I discovered the tremendous power of living on mission with purpose. I realized that leadership is not simply about guiding others; it is also about inspiring them to discover and maximize their own potential, to build a legacy that will endure long after they are gone, to leave the world a better place when they exit it than when they entered it.

On Mission with Purpose is more than a book—it is an invitation. Each chapter thoughtfully explores a critical theme that defines a life of significance. The journey begins with the foundational question: What is purpose? Through personal stories and practical insights, Steven will guide you to reflect on what purpose means to you and how it serves as your anchor even in turbulent times. The book then illuminates the benefits of living with purpose, showing how clarity and conviction catalyze both personal fulfillment and organizational success.

One of the most powerful truths I have learned over many decades is that resistance is not an obstacle, but a necessity. In facing adversity, our purpose is tested and refined. God uses the fire of adversity to mold us, to refine us, and to make something beautiful from the ashes. The chapters on resistance and the quest for contentment are especially relevant today, as so many leaders struggle with burnout and the pressure to always do more. Here, you will find encouragement to embrace challenges as opportunities for growth and to seek a deeper sense of contentment—not in the absence of struggle, but in the presence of meaning.

As the book unfolds, the conversation expands from purpose to meaning, exploring the distinction and the deep connection between the two. What is meaning? How do we find it, and how do we help others discover it for themselves? These chapters will challenge you to think deeply about your leadership and the legacy you are building.

Success is often unpredictable, and the pursuit of success can be both exhilarating and exhausting. Yet, as you will read, true mission-driven leaders are those who serve a cause greater than themselves. The exploration of mission—whom do you serve and why?—will inspire you to recalibrate your priorities. For those of us who serve God, there is a profound calling to steward our God-given gifts and influence for the greater good.

A particularly resonant message in this book is the call to "don't retire; recalibrate." In a world obsessed with titles and achievements, it is refreshing to be reminded that our greatest contributions often come after we have reached traditional milestones. The path to significance does not end; and sometimes it is just beginning at retirement age. Our mission continues, and our legacy is built not in a moment but in a lifetime of purposeful action. Mentoring others is a critical step of living a purpose-driven life.

As you embark on this journey through the pages of ***On Mission with Purpose***, I encourage you to pause, reflect, and embrace the challenges and invitations within. Whether you are a seasoned leader or just beginning to explore God's calling on your life, this book will equip you with the insights, tools, and encouragement needed to live and lead with intention. Now more than ever, the world needs leaders who are unwavering in their commitment to purpose—leaders who not only seek to be successful but also are intentional to be significant.

May this book inspire you as much as it has inspired me. May you discover your unique mission, and may you build a legacy that makes the world a better place for generations to come.

Mark Whitacre, PhD

Vice President, Culture & Care

Executive Director of Transformation-Factor

Coca-Cola Consolidated

FROM PURPOSE TO MEANING TO MISSION

Vision sees the stars; mission carves the path to reach them. Vision without a purposeful mission is a ship without a compass, drifting aimlessly in the sea of aspirations.[1] –Aloo Denish Obiero

For most of my life, I thought I knew what my purpose was. I was in great part wrong. I confused what I did for a living and my career with why I am alive and what I was called to do. I realized God was connected in some way to my life's purpose and mission but could not define what they were. As a result, at times I sacrificed what the Bible calls the peace that *surpasses all understanding* for an offset version of what I had decided I was called to do instead of what God actually called me to do. Even so, I prayed often for God to help me discover His unique purpose and mission for my life.

Western culture typically defines purpose and mission in terms of performance, worldly success, power, influence, and material wealth. For the most part, I guarded against that secular idea of purpose and mission because I knew God had something much greater in mind for me. He defines our purpose and mission through meaning and significance in relation to His ways and eternal plan. It may seem weird that the God of the universe would have a plan from eternity for each of us as individuals, but He does (Jeremiah 29:11–12; Genesis 1:27–28; Psalm 139:16; Proverbs 19:21). If not careful, we risk conflating the world's idea with God's plan. In my case, the peace of God patiently sat on the sideline as He allowed me to pursue my ideas over His. This was nobody's fault but my own.

I finally recognized that I was getting ahead of God with my plans after a long year of sprinting toward the finish line in my busiest season, which starts in September and goes through mid-December. I was waking up every night with pressure on my chest, a mind that sped faster than a NASCAR racecar, and a weight of responsibility on my life that I could no longer hold up or carry. I knew the only way back to finding rest, peace, provision, and purpose was to return to my first love. As Jesus said through John to the church in Ephesus, *"But I have this against you, that you have abandoned the love you had at first. Remember therefore from where you have fallen; repent, and do the works you did at first. If not, I will come to you and remove your lampstand from its place, unless you repent"* (Revelation 2:4–5).

With nothing else to give, I prayed daily and received clear direction from God, which was to do fewer things but do them better rather than do more things faster and with a lack of contemplation. For two months, I sat in my office with an empty tank, reading the Bible, listening to sermons, and reading books written by godly men who had been where I was at in that moment. I cut four major programs and objectives from my ministry and began focusing on where I believed the Lord was leading me. At first I was reluctant, because while it's true that purpose gives us meaning, without putting my purpose and meaning into actional mission, it was like owning a beautiful Lamborghini but never driving it. What good is that car if I don't put it to use?

And thus birthed a time of growth, refocus, and an anticipation for what the Lord had next for me. It was a difficult time, but I was adamant about remaining teachable and making the changes in my life and ministry God called me to. This process led me to examine the relationship of a healthy, God-led understanding of a life of purpose and meaning, lived out in a fulfilling mission.

Purpose, meaning, and mission go hand in hand. If you lack one of them, you miss all of them. When you have a sense of purpose, your optimism, hope, resiliency, perseverance, and most of all, your joy increase. Reaching one's true purpose in life demands a defined level of meaning and mission. It's like baking a cake. There are five necessary ingredients for making and baking a basic cake: flour, salt, butter, sugar, and water. While many other ingredients can be added, these are the essential ones. Now imagine trying to bake a cake without flour, water, or salt. Stick that incomplete mixture into the oven and bake it for the perfect amount of time. After it's cooled, take a big bite and let me know how you like it.

In this book I will break down the three basic categories for baking the cake of a vibrant, purposeful life: purpose, meaning, and mission. I will use both contemporary and ancient wisdom, dating back thousands of years, in an effort to provide a 365-degree view of what you and I need to do to live a satisfying life driven by purpose, meaning, and mission. This is what I call the "Trifecta: The Power of Purpose to Meaning to Mission." Having a shallow or artificial life purpose is not a true purpose at all and eventually fizzles out. Why? Because an artificial purpose cannot sustain the need for human meaning and mission. When difficult times pop up in one's life, an artificial cause leads to a false meaning, which leads to an artificial purpose. And an artificial purpose is not worth the risk because it involves living out a false mission.

The ancient psalmist said this of life purpose: *I cry out to God Most High, to God who fulfills his purpose for me* (Psalm 57:2). In this verse, King David took refuge in God because he trusted God to show him the way to complete the mission at hand. David knew the meaning and purpose of his life, but at that time the mission looked bleak.

Like David who knew that his purpose would be fulfilled, the ancient character Saul of Tarsus, whose name was changed to Paul, said this: *And we know that for those who love God all things work together for good, for those who are called according to his purpose* (Romans 8:28). In other words, we can have short- and long-term purpose, meaning, and mission. For example, military missions have short-term battles. But those battles fit within a larger war. Businesspeople win large contracts, but those contracts fit within the larger business as a whole. Parents have a short mission of eighteen years to raise their children with love, direction, godliness, and wisdom to prepare them to live life independently.

The reason we do anything is because we hope for a specific outcome. And it's within that spirit we jump into discovering what it means to live a life full of meaning, purpose, and mission. A purpose-driven life is birthed out of a good (not evil) cause or meaning, which in turn materializes as good actions through meaningful mission. For example, if a person's purpose is to rob banks and become rich, the focus of the mission carries zero or no meaning because it's presumably based on gaining wealth. If the bank robber is caught and put into prison, his prison time becomes unrelated or disconnected to the mission itself. As a result, prison time (a by-product of the evil mission) becomes irrelevant to the purpose and meaning of their mission. On the flip side, if one is put in prison for their faith, their mission is more often than not enriched, as difficult as that might seem. Why? Their mission has depth and meaning because it helps other human beings and reflects God's calling.

The mission of sharing one's faith carries the risk of persecution as a scary but real consequence. The Christian faith adds the element of God's hand being upon those who suffer for their faith to sustain them, but even a nonreligious purpose can lead to a reasonable level of meaning and mission that can carry one through difficult circumstances.

Around 935 BC, the ancient sage King Solomon wrote this: *Vanity of vanities, says the Preacher, vanity of vanities! All is vanity. What does man gain by all his toils under the sun?* (Ecclesiastes 1:2–3). Solomon later wrote, *There is nothing better for a person than that he should eat and drink and find enjoyment in his toil. This also, I saw, is from the hand of God* (Ecclesiastes 2:24). Another Bible version translates the verse this way: *So I decided there is nothing better than to enjoy food and drink and to find satisfaction in work. Then I realized that these pleasures are from the hand of God* (Ecclesiastes 2:24 NLT).

When writing my first book in 2011, my wife asked me an interesting question: "Why are you writing this book?" The book was titled *Right for You, But Not for Me: A Response to Moral Relativism*. At the time, I knew the reason for writing that book: Morality is behind every issue and topic, ranging from sex to politics to business to marriage and life in every aspect you can imagine.

Fast-forward over twenty years and ask me again, "Steve, why are you writing a book on purpose, meaning, and mission?" It all started two years ago when my wife Heather and I were talking about my next book. She has been hounding me for more than two years to write this book. Why? Because after twenty-five years of marriage, she knows me. She knows what makes me tick, and she knows that my clear, consistent calling is to bring hope to others. But underneath all that, Heather also knows, as I do, that hope is an essential driver of our mission. As Billy Graham said, "Perhaps the greatest psychological, spiritual, and medical need that all people have is the need for hope."[2] Heather and I have an eternal hope in God through Jesus Christ. That drives all we do. But it's our hope that drives us to seek and fulfill the specific purpose for our lives, which in turn gives us true meaning which drives our mission.

That is the reason I started TriedstonePublishing.com, EquippedAcademy.com, and ReasonForTruth.org. It's not only our hope for the eternal but also a hope for our present temporal life. We live in a difficult time in world history. But as I will address later in the book, these difficulties, challenges, and setbacks make the journey worthwhile. Resistance causes our life purpose to surface, unveiling true meaning and what we are called to do about our purpose, which is to live out our mission. That is the focus of and my goal for this book: to help you discover your purpose, meaning, and mission in life.

When many of us consider who some of the most successful people in our culture are, we tend to think of financially successful individuals such as Jeff Bezos and Elon Musk. They are hyper-focused people who understand why they do what they do and have a strong sense of purpose in the marketplace. That drives them to know how to go to market and make things happen (the mission). But not everyone gets to be the founder of Amazon or Tesla. For most of us, success is defined in a different way, on a very different level.

Austrian psychiatrist and Holocaust survivor Viktor E. Frankl said, "If you don't know what your mission in life is, you already have one—to find it."[3] In this book, we are going to discover and connect the journey from purpose to meaning to mission to help you discover how you can best live out your life to the greatest potential. But we cannot separate ultimate purpose, meaning, and mission from an Ultimate Authority (God) who commissions us. Whether you are religious or not, you will find this book extremely insightful and essential in helping you discover your clear purpose and mission in our confused world.

By sharing some of my mistakes, I hope to guide you through your process of discovering God and His purpose in a deeper way. By reading this book, you are helping me fulfill my purpose, meaning, and mission, which includes offering you what God has taught me. I hope you will read it all the way to the end. Thank you for entrusting your time, mind, and heart to discover the importance of finding, embracing, and living out your life of purpose with meaning and mission.

—Steven Garofalo

1

WHAT IS PURPOSE?

The Purpose of your life is to participate in the ultimate cosmic drama-working with God to cultivate heaven on earth.
– J. Raynor[4]

In 1988 a massive earthquake hit Armenia, killing twenty-five thousand people. After the initial shock set in, one father remembered his promise to his son Armon: "No matter what, I'll always be there for you!" Armon had gone to school that morning, so the father ran to the building to find his eight-year-old son. Upon arrival, the father found the school demolished. This is where the father's mission came in, but not before purpose and meaning set the foundation for that mission. The purpose was to find his son, dead or alive. The meaning was his promise to his son. The mission was to keep that promise.

Armon's father arrived and started to dig through the debris with his hands. The police told him to go home because his mission was futile. There was no sign of life. But the father was on a mission with purpose and did not even consider abandoning it. He shifted his search to an area where he thought his son's classroom had been.

He dug for eight hours with no help. Eight hours turned into twelve, then to twenty-four. Other parents saw his determination and joined his mission, as hopeless as it seemed. During the thirty-eighth hour, he pulled away a heavy piece of rubble and heard, "Dad? It's me! I told the other kids not to worry. I told them that if you were still alive, you'd save me, and when you saved me, they'd be saved. You promised, 'No matter what, I'll always be there for you! You did it, Dad!"

Fourteen scared, hungry, thirsty children were saved by a tent-like pocket of concrete. Can you imagine what those children would have gone through and how the lives of their surviving families would have changed if Armon's father had not taken on his daily mission with purpose despite such dismal odds?[5]

Like Armon's father, you and I make decisions about purpose and mission every morning before we start our day—every one of us, whether we're ten or a hundred years old, famous or unknown, rich or poor. We all have life purpose and mission. And when we live out our purpose through mission, we gain the riches of true meaning. So, I want to start our journey in this discovery with purpose.

MAKING MONEY VS. FULFILLING PURPOSE

Growing up, I loved to watch television like most people did in the 1960s and '70s. My favorite show was *Flipper*. This popular family adventure centered on a bottlenose dolphin and his friends in a marine preserve located in the Florida Keys. The series' eighty episodes captivated me.

Why bring up this childhood memory? I have always been drawn to the water and a more laid-back lifestyle. After watching a 1967 television episode of the show *Flipper* one day as a boy under the age of ten, I asked my brother, "Why do people work so hard so they can afford to do things like go on vacation in the Florida Keys when they can live full-time in the Florida Keys and not work so hard for most of their lives?"

He said, "Steven, no place is perfect and no life is perfect. If you live in the Florida Keys, you have extreme heat in the summer and the yearly possibility that a hurricane can destroy everything you have." He was correct. There is no utopia in our current world. But his reality check left a gaping hole in my quest to fulfill my dream of life by the water. I got my scuba diving license at age thirteen, in great part because my other brother made that possible. But despite that achievement and my love for the water, I never ended up living in the Florida Keys. But I do not regret the loss. Why? Living a life of purpose, meaning, and mission—and enjoying it—is a process that involves God and a resolve to accept that He has a plan for our lives (Ecclesiastes 5:18), which may not include what we desire or dream of.

Most every human being longs to discover and live out their God-given purpose. That purpose might be a seemingly small or short event or a long, drawn-out process. Either way, our purpose gives us joy and fulfillment. That purpose-driven joy and fulfillment give us meaning, and that meaning drives us to act on and live out our life purpose in verb-form mission.

In past years, the world (and life in general) was much simpler. Most people had a job, worked that job, then went home and ate dinner with their family. Today, with the advent of technology and large companies becoming publicly traded, humans have become commodities and tools designed for profit. A consequence of our modern age is increased corruption and greed, and such progressive greed is leading people to desire becoming rich quickly over a principled purpose-driven mission calling they were designed for. As a result, what matters most in life—namely God, family, and a more balanced lifestyle—has been sacrificed on the altar of materialism. And a purpose-driven missional life has been sacrificed on that altar. Overwhelmingly, people reject any form of delayed gratification and live for money and prestige, which only satisfy for a short time. I want to help you begin to turn that around for our generation and the next. I am reminded of 1 Timothy 6:10 which says, *For the love of money is a root of all kinds of evils. It is through this craving that some have wandered away from the faith and pierced themselves with many pangs.*

In truth, money in and of itself is not a problem—but the love of money is. Love of money is a root, though not the root of evil. The ancient king Solomon, the wealthiest and most powerful man in the world in his lifetime, wrote: *Whoever loves money never has enough; whoever loves wealth is never satisfied with their income. This too is meaningless* (Ecclesiastes 5:10 NIV).

In *The Top 10 Reasons the Rich Go Broke,* CFP, author, and speaker John MacGregor writes, "I've worked with countless individuals through the years, from those struggling to find financial footing to those deemed 'well-off' by general society. In my experience, the level of wealth or income didn't matter much because, in fact, everyone has the exact same problem when it comes to money. Most people today use money to dull their pain rather than fulfill their purpose." [6]

What does this have to do with purpose, meaning, and mission? Everything. Let's start by looking at what we can fulfill our life purpose with, if not money.

Our life purpose is a journey developed throughout our entire life. It is formed through an eternal calling which allows for good and bad times, because all things will be worked together for our good as we pursue discovering and living out our life purpose.

PURPOSE AND OUR LIFE STORY

Purpose starts with understanding where you come from. Whether you come from a good place or a bad one, it's essential to understand your origin because your past has played a major role in making you who you are today. All of us prefer to take the good and leave the bad, but the bad can also be used for good.

In *The Transformation Factor,* Coca-Cola Bottling Co. Consolidated CEO J. Frank Harrison III wrote, "Like it or not, our purpose in life is wrapped up in our entire life's story. In order to determine why you're here and what you're supposed to do, you also have to consider who you were, who you are, and who you're becoming."[7] Harrison recounts the start of Coca-Cola in Atlanta, Georgia, back in 1891. Pharmacist John Pemberton created the first batch of Coca-Cola in a drug store before another pharmacist by the name of Asa Candler acquired all rights to the business for $2,300. In 1892, Candler formed what is now known as The Coca-Cola Company.

Under Mr. Candler's leadership, Coca-Cola was being sold all over the southeastern United States. In 1899, Ben Thomas and Joseph Whitehead bought the franchise rights to bottle Coke for the entire U.S. for $1 from Mr. Candler. Those rights were in perpetuity, and soon small Coke manufacturing and distribution plants sprang up across the United States, from California to New York selling one product—6.5-oz. bottles of Coca-Cola.

Coca-Cola Consolidated went public in the 1970s and by the late 1970s the company grew to include Coke, Fanta, Sprite, Mellow Yellow, and Fresca. Today, the company covers fourteen states and the District of Columbia and delivers more than 300 different products to almost 20 percent of the U.S. public.[8] The current state of Coca-Cola Consolidated and who J. Frank Harrison and his family are today were impacted and formed by where he and his family came from. And that past, present, and future vision are guided, if not directed, by one thing: purpose. Harrison's life is driven solely by purpose, which in turn drives the company to be driven by purpose as well.

Case in point. Harrison says Coca-Cola Consolidated has a purpose to drive culture, and that culture is based on their purpose, or as he says, why they are here on earth. More specifically, the company's stated purpose is to "honor God with all they do, to serve others, to pursue excellence, and to grow profitably." Harrison believes there is nothing more important—not even money. If they get the culture right, they will do incredibly well as a business, as people, and as a company. Furthermore, to honor God in all they do is clearly connected to their values. Truth and integrity are everything. If there is no truth, there is no trust. If there is no trust, there is no relationship.

Putting other people first takes humility. Harrison says that serving others is very important and that the most important person is the servant. He also says that selling Coca-Cola Consolidated products is about serving others, and if you serve others, you won't be able to build enough plants to handle the volume. In other words, living out our true, eternal purpose leads to success in ways we may never have expected. Additionally, the element of purpose includes doing things with excellence, which helps lead to genuine growth. There is no real purpose in a static-driven life. Harrison says that growth is good and growth is godly. If we are not growing as individuals, that's a problem. The same is true of any company. Companies must grow their people, because the company won't grow unless their people grow.[9]

I may never have accomplished my life dream of owning a pet dolphin like Flipper or living on the water, but God has blessed me with a beautiful, godly wife and three children who seek the Lord with all their heart, mind, life, and soul. As it turns out, in great part, they are a major part of my life purpose and mission. God has provided for me and my family in ways I cannot explain. For example, after the 2008 GFC (Great Financial Collapse), He provided the work that allowed my wife to homeschool our three children and for me to go to seminary as well as start a ministry, a business, and publish multiple books. In the process, God taught me how to better put others before myself.

All this has not only given me greater life purpose but also improved my physical health. Nobody can believe my age when I tell them. Recently, I had the privilege of spending a week with my two older brothers in Costa Rica, where my oldest brother now lives. A funny moment occurred when they said, "How do you have all your hair … and it's still dark?" I chuckled and quoted as best I could the minor prophet Joel who wrote, *"I [God]will restore to you the years that the swarming locust has eaten, the hopper, the destroyer, and the cutter, my great army, which I sent among you"* (Joel 2:24). In other words, the Lord has restored a level of youth to me for me, in turn, to use for His glory and life mission. I complimented my oldest brother on living out his Christian faith in mission as I sought to do the same, noting that living with purpose is directly related to a longer, more physically healthy life. That's what we look at next, as we begin the journey of discovering what purpose is and how we can live out our purpose, which leads to a life of meaning and mission.

2

THE BENEFITS OF PURPOSE

Our world is obsessed with success. But how does God define success?
Success in God's eyes is faithfulness to His calling.
– Billy Graham[10]

In the job I had for over seven years prior to moving to Charlotte, North Carolina, I was working at a recruiting and assessment company as Vice President of Operations and Special Projects in the Washington D.C. area. I was driving home from work one day, tuning in a bit late to Hank Hanegraaff's *Bible Answer Man* radio program when I heard "This is perhaps one of the best seminaries in the world. … No, it's the very best seminary in the world."

I reached around to pull out a pen and something to write down the name of this seminary, but then Hank said, "I will tell you all about it when we return from this commercial break." I pulled over, found a pen and piece of paper, and prayed, "God, I realize this seminary couldn't be in Charlotte as Charlotte is a small city, but if this seminary could be in Atlanta, GA, I could commute for summer modules and perhaps study at a distance."

Around that same time, my future wife Heather and I were on a three-day singles church beach retreat. In the first two days, unsolicited, different friends stopped me three times and said, "We were talking, and you need to go to seminary." One of them was Heather! My main obstacle at that time was the few number of seminaries in the D.C. area. Also, the traffic congestion would make it extremely difficult for me to commute to both work and school.

When the commercial break ended, Hank said the seminary was located in Charlotte, NC. I almost fell out of the seat of my car. When I got home, I ordered the book of courses and packed it away.

About a year and a half later, Heather and I married and moved to Charlotte. I plugged the address of the seminary into a new thing called Yahoo Maps, and it came up 6.5 miles from my house. In 1999, there was little if any traffic in Charlotte, so God removed all obstacles to enrolling in seminary because it was His will, His calling, and part of His purpose and mission for me.

When Heather and I moved to Charlotte, we selected a house, which we sold a year later to move onto two acres in the country. People in my office back in the D.C. area took bets on how long I would last. The shortest bet was three weeks. As I write this book, my family has lived in that second house twenty-six years. This house is only 2.5 miles from the seminary. I guess God wanted to get through my head that He heard my concerns.

Horses trotted down our street when we first moved in. Not something you see in the D.C. area unless it's the D.C. police or a dignitary's funeral. Life was slower, and in some ways a bit boring. But that allowed me to slow down, think, pray more deeply, and use what started off as boredom as a conduit to a deeper relationship with God, my wife, and the seminary. I even became president of my class. Sometimes God brings us through seasons of stillness, introspective thought, and yes, even boredom in an effort to slow us down and recalibrate our relationship with Him. Boredom is one of the many tools God uses in helping us discover and live out our purpose and mission.

In *Redeeming Your Time* Jordan Raymond writes, "As we've seen, boredom doesn't come naturally for us in the twenty-first century, so we have to intentionally develop the skill of being bored."[11] In one study, a significant percentage of participants—67 percent of men and 25 percent of women—preferred to administer electric shocks to themselves rather than experience boredom while sitting alone with their thoughts.[12] Simply put, living a life of boredom, void of purpose and resistance, is not a recipe for a long, healthy life.

On the contrary, people with a solid life purpose tend to live longer. For example, Reverend Billy Graham lived to age ninety-nine and Mother Teresa to age eighty-seven. Bob Hope, George Burns, and Gloria Stuart all lived to be 100 years or older. While there is no causal connection between one's retirement and their death, studies show that mortality rates tend to increase shortly after retirement. This can be attributed to numerous factors, including a decline in physical activity, changes in social life and interaction with others, and even stress derived from such a major life change. Think about the cycle of life. After living out your youngest years, you get married and raise children, which provides significant purpose. You go to work, which gives you further purpose for the next season of your adulthood.

Then you wake up one day, and you are in retirement or semi-retirement. Sadly, at this point some people find themselves getting up, eating breakfast, watching TV, and taking the dog for a walk as the center of their life. While that may sound good, it doesn't sharpen your mind, body, or heart. What sharpens your mind, body, and soul is some form or resistance. Physically speaking, that resistance means physical exercise. Mentally speaking, that means reading, doing puzzles, and volunteering your time to solve problems and give back to society.

I'm not putting down retirement, only misdirected retirement. Retirement can be the most fulfilling period of your journey for living out a purpose-led life. In this season, your kids are grown up and out of college, which leaves many financially set. Furthermore, most people have the extra time they didn't have when they were younger as they don't work full-time and have raised their children. These retirement years are an opportune time to give back to others, especially the younger generation and a local church. There is no shortage of those in need, such as single mothers and the elderly. And people with purpose tend to be much healthier and sharper, and they live longer. (More on retirement and purpose in chapter 14.)

WHY PEOPLE WITH PURPOSE LIVE LONGER AND BETTER

In "Purposeful People Live Longer—and Better—According to Research," published in *The Epoch Times*, Dr. Yuhong Dong says that scientists discovered that a person who finds positive meaning in their life affects their life positively. In the article, "life purpose is defined as having purpose in life and being responsible for one's own actions."[13] Experts in psychosomatic medicine recommended it as an important factor in promoting mental health and increasing one's resilience.

Furthermore, the more purposeful one's life is, the better and stronger one's immune system is. A study was conducted in 2003 by Dr. Julienne Bower and her team of researchers at the UCLA Department of Psychiatry and Biobehavioral Sciences. This four-week study included forty-three females who had recently lost a close relative, their mother in most cases, to breast cancer. The article noted that the grief from the loss of one's loved one can cause the release of stress hormones, which in turn decrease immune functions and the body's ability to fight viruses and diseases such as cancer. These participants were found to be at high risk of breast cancer.[14]

The research team concluded that the probability of one getting breast cancer is related to one's thoughts. But those in the study who started to actively search for the purpose of life had stronger Natural Killer (NK) cell functions, which led to a decreased risk of breast cancer. The research team also concluded that the philosophical (and I would submit the theological) topic of life purpose has a direct relationship to our cells' immune function. The study found that both searching and thinking about the purpose of life can not only strengthen the immune cells but also influence the body as a whole and its other functions.

In the end, I don't believe we can discover true life purpose without God because He is the Creator of all things. You and I were created by something much greater than ourselves, and that something is God. Because He is our Creator, God knows exactly how we are put together, and He knows us better than we know ourselves. Psalm 139:13 says, *For you created my inmost being; you knit me together in my mother's womb* (NIV). As our Creator, God knit us together from eternity with a life purpose as He works all things together in our lives for His glory (Romans 8:28).

In *The Purpose-Driven Life*, Rick Warren wrote, "The purpose of your life is far greater than your own personal fulfillment, your peace of mind, or even your happiness. It's far greater than your family, your career, or even your wildest dreams and ambitions. If you want to know why you were placed on this planet, you must begin with God. You were born by his purpose and for his purpose."[15]

THE BENEFIT OF PURPOSE IN THE MARKETPLACE

In the marketplace, growth and success are generally defined in terms of temporal things such as power, position, recognition, material possessions, and wealth. If we're honest with ourselves, these are all short-term achievements in our temporal world and short lifespan. But worldly achievements, success, and growth are truly fulfilling only when they are lived out properly in light of our true life purpose. When we attempt to live a life of purpose for wrong, selfish reasons, we turn our purpose-driven, meaningful life in a meaningless direction. This is why having a God-inspired vision, purpose, and meaning are essential in differentiating a value-added mission.

Having a proper vision and purpose will ultimately lead you to a life of significance, meaning and purpose. When power, recognition, material possessions and wealth are viewed from a biblical perspective, they become by-products and wonderful tools as God's provision to us as opposed to the selfish, mislabeled resources we create. When we keep our priorities straight, God leads us to a compelling vision and purpose in life, family, work, and business. And this is the importance of discovering and living out our true purpose, meaning, and mission in the world, our family, among our friends, and in the marketplace.[16]

Having a God-inspired vision for meaning and purpose is essential to your personal life, to your family, and for your mission in the marketplace. A God-inspired purpose for you and your organization will lead to becoming a value-added, morally reputable person and organization. This in turn will separate you from your competition, which is growing increasingly immoral according to God's absolute Moral Law. As illustrated in chapter 1 through Coca-Cola Consolidated CEO J. Frank Harrison's words, having a vision and purpose will expand your personal mission and any organization's definition of growth and success to one of greater significance, meaning, and purpose. For many, this will entail moving from making money as their main focus to making a value-added difference in the lives of others, namely your customers and employees in the marketplace. The money will follow. Matthew 6:33 tells us, *But seek first his kingdom and his righteousness, and all these things will be given to you as well* (NIV).

In *The Road Ahead* Bill Gates wrote, "Success is a lousy teacher. It seduces smart people into thinking they can't lose."[17] But when we keep our priorities straight, God leads us to a compelling vision and purpose in life, family, work, and business.

GOD HAS SHAPED YOU WITH PURPOSE

God has shaped and prepared you to play a unique role in each step of your life story. Each one of us has a purpose designed to bring glory to God if we are faithful and obedient and carry out that purpose into motion through mission. Defining purpose benefits both individuals and organizations in the marketplace alike. Most of us at one time or another have asked ourselves what the meaning of life is and what our meaning and purpose in this life is. As Rick Warren so eloquently said, it all starts with God. The more difficult thing is discovering what our life purpose is.

FINDING PURPOSE IN LIFE

How do we find our life purpose? A good starting point is the Westminster Catechism, which states that the chief purpose of mankind is "to glorify God, and to enjoy him forever (1 Cor. 10:31; Rom. 11:36; Ps. 73:25–28)." Our purpose in life (and in the marketplace), as God originally created man (and woman) is fourfold: 1) Glorifying God and enjoying fellowship with Him; 2) Cultivating and maintaining healthy relationships with others; 3) Working and finding fulfillment in what God calls us to do; and 4) Having dominion over the earth, which means being good stewards of the earth by not abusing it. These four goals are a good starting point for discovering God's purpose for our life. When we enjoy God by following His purpose for our lives, we are able to experience true and lasting joy—the abundant life He desires for us.

Our life purpose is found by anchoring life in God's glory through obedience to Scriptures and cultivating our delight in Him as opposed to focusing strictly on our self-centered goals. When we make our daily life a reflection of God and His divine nature, our life purpose will be clarified and fulfilled in ways we never imagined. Let's look more closely at the four ways to find our life purpose listed above.

First, glorify God and enjoy fellowship with Him. This is the chief purpose of our human existence. To glorify God is to honor Him in all we do in all our actions. By doing so, we find ultimate joy in His presence. By living out purpose in mission and action, coupled with fellowship with Christ through prayer and studying His Word, God shows us His ways, which are the best ways to live. As a result, God transforms our daily life into a form of worship. This is why God created us as man and woman, and it is the first way to help us discover our purpose.

Second, cultivate and maintain healthy relationships with others. This way of discovering purpose has been greatly stressed since the COVID-19 crisis, because so many relationships are transitioning from personal to digital. But people are not digital; we are relational. Cultivating healthy relationships is crucial for Christ-followers as a primary command from God to love others.

In regard to the greatest commandment, Jesus said, *"You shall love the Lord your God with all your heart and with all your soul and with all your mind. This is the great and first commandment. And a second is like it: You shall love your neighbor as yourself. On these two commandments depend all the Law and the Prophets"* (Matthew 23:37–40). Our personal relationships and connections are modeled after Jesus's self-sacrificial, patient, and unconditional love. Relationships are essential to our spiritual growth, and accountability is part of the journey of finding our life purpose through service, spiritual development, and helping others.

Third, work and find fulfillment in what God calls us to do. No matter what our work, or better yet our labor, involves it is a divine calling to serve God not just other people. Colossians 3:23 says, *Whatever you do, work heartily, as for the Lord and not for men.* By working to the glory of God with diligence and integrity to the best of our ability, we learn to treat tasks, which always include or affect other people, as a form of worship to God. However simple or dull they may be, we as Christ followers find purpose in our tasks because all good acts of service ultimately honor God and others.

Fourth, we are to exercise dominion over the entire earth. This does not mean we are to destroy the earth in the process of establishing dominion; rather we are to be good stewards by nurturing, not abusing it. This last goal for discovering God's purpose for our lives comes right out of Genesis 1:26–28:

> *Then God said, "Let us make man in our image, after our likeness. And let them have dominion over the fish of the sea and over the birds of the heavens and over the livestock and over all the earth and*

> *over every creeping thing that creeps on the earth." So God created man in his own image, in the image of God he created him; male and female he created them. And God blessed them. And God said to them, "Be fruitful and multiply and fill the earth and subdue it, and have dominion over the fish of the sea and over the birds of the heavens and over every living thing that moves on the earth."*

Good stewardship means managing earth's resources for human good and God's glory, representing His reign rather than exploiting or abusing the planet. In the end, our dominion over the earth gives us a foundational purpose by uniquely empowering humans (not animals) to cultivate the earth directly under God's authority, using the resources He has provided for the good of others, not just ourselves. From raising crops to designing and building a hospital, from delivering mail to being a sanitation worker—all these tasks glorify God. And doing so helps us discover our life purpose.

IN THE QUIET MOMENTS

As I mentioned earlier, God used times of quiet, to redirect me toward my life purpose and mission. I am reminded of Elijah, who sought God in the noisiness of life but found Him in the quiet whisper.

> *The Lord said, "Go out and stand on the mountain in the presence of the Lord, for the Lord is about to pass by." Then a great and powerful wind tore the mountains apart and shattered the rocks before the Lord, but the Lord was not in the wind. After the wind there was an earthquake, but the Lord was not in the earthquake. After the earthquake came a fire, but the Lord was not in the fire. And after the fire came a gentle whisper. When Elijah heard it, he pulled his cloak over his face and went out and stood at the mouth of the cave. Then a voice said to him, "What are you doing here, Elijah?"* (1 Kings 19:11–13 NIV).

Elijah doesn't find God in the noise of powerful wind, earthquake, or fire, but in the silence, or better yet, in God's *gentle whisper*. In that moment, God spoke to Elijah. It's often in the silence that God speaks to us in a quiet, intimate way rather than a loud, flashy display, urging us to succumb to the need to be still in order to hear His voice. And from there, God's purpose begins to become clearer.

The benefits of having a defined purpose in life and in the marketplace are multifaceted and numerous. Living with purpose tends to give clarity to people and to corporations. Bill Gates was correct when he said that success is a lousy teacher because it seduces smart people into thinking they can't lose. Such a prideful, self-sufficient attitude doesn't help us discover and live out our purpose in life and in the marketplace. Desiring to discover and live out our purpose and mission in a way that brings glory to God does. This entails being faithful and obedient to God and carrying out that purpose into motion through mission. This is a journey that includes good times, bad times, and working through some resistance. And this is what we discover in the next chapter. By overcoming obstacles, we become more purpose-driven and stronger.

3

THE NECESSITY OF RESISTENCE

A muscle becomes weak if it is not used.
To become strong, a muscle must push against something.
–Billy Graham[19]

My father was born and raised, until about eight years of age, in Pozzallo, Sicily, Italy. He later worked hard to become an electrical engineer for the Department of the Navy in the 1960s. My mother was amazing on every level in every area of living—from home-cooked meals to accepting nothing less than a neat, orderly home from all of us. When my father died of a heart attack in 1970, my mother was thrown into raising four children alone: my sister who was seven days old, me at age five, and my two older brothers, who were nine and eleven at the time. Talk about facing resistance.

Three years later, my mother was diagnosed with late-stage leukemia and given six months to live. A Catholic priest came into her room at N. I. H. (National Institute of Health) in Washington, DC, read her the Last Rites, then told her to get her papers in order and her children positioned to be cared for by others as there was no hope for her survival.

Within twenty-four hours, my father's brother, my uncle John, came down from New Jersey, picked her up, and took her to Sloan and Kettering, a world-renowned comprehensive cancer center in New

York City. She was given the last-resort option of a new, experimental chemotherapy, which she accepted. My sister, age three, went to live with my grandparents in Brooklyn, New York, while my brothers and I stayed with different neighbors within one street of one another for six months. Talk about long-term guests!

A man by the name of Ron wanted to marry my mom, which was the only viable option for keeping her children together, as no one relative or friend could or would take four orphans. Each Friday, Ron picked up my two older brothers and me, then drove us three and half hours to New York City to stay with my grandparents. When my mother was not too sick from chemotherapy, we visited her in the hospital.

Six months later, my mother was released from the hospital in remission. She was written up in *The New York Times* as a miracle story. Her two doctors were top in their field in the world. One doctor said the new chemotherapy was the most amazing cure they had found for cancer yet. The second doctor, a professing Christian, said, "No, if the cancer didn't kill her, the experimental chemotherapy should have" because the level of very crude experimental chemotherapy back in the 1970s was three times the dose they should have given her.

When my mom came home, she gathered us four kids around her for a family meeting, where she stated clearly and emphatically that she was too weak to do everything she had previously done in the home. Each of us had to take personal responsibility—do our assigned chores and clean up after ourselves—if we were to survive and stay together as a family. The room was quiet. From my oldest brother down to my four-year-old sister, there was no complaining, no crying, and no regret—just thankfulness that we had our mother and one another.

After that meeting, our home worked like clockwork. We were an A-team, not out of obligation but out of love, respect, and mission to stay together—not to simply survive but to thrive. And we did. In spite of all that resistance, we thrived as a family. No whining, nobody riding on the back of other family members. Just solid family teamwork. And while not perfect, my upbringing was about as good as one can experience. The resistance shaped us into a strong, close, and accomplished family.

ESSENTIAL RESISTANCE

Resistance is the ability to withstand or oppose external forces or pressures that threaten a person, organization, system, or group. It often plays a crucial role in understanding how individuals respond to problematic situations, and it involves challenges such as social change, oppression, politics, and adversity. Resistance comes in various forms, ranging from personal trials and conflicts to advancements such as job promotion and other positive changes. These internal or external pushbacks usually involve struggle, change, growth, and discomfort. While resistance can be uncomfortable, it leads to transformative changes in life and spiritual growth.

Resistance is necessary to make you strong—physically, mentally, and spiritually. While physical fitness and strength training builds muscle by working against force, mental and spiritual growth occur only through overcoming life challenges that by default build resilience, character, inner fortitude, and most importantly faith in God. In any case, when our capacity in any of these areas is challenged, our default or existing strength capacity or level leads to adaptation and increased strength, whether that be stronger muscles, bones, mental acuity, a more resilient mind, or a stronger faith in God.

Resistance is not only necessary in discovering your purpose but also unavoidable in living out your mission. By resistance, I mean that we will run into pushback from people, organizations, nature, and all other facets of life. For example, when you live out your mission, you will encounter people who are envious or jealous of your focus, joy, excitement, energy, and mission. At some point, you will have to push through and go around, over, underneath, or through that obstacle or person. I don't mean physical resistance unless you are faced with a life-or-death situation. In most cases, persevering through resistance will come in the form of political obstacles and interpersonal friction that we face when achieving success through mission with purpose. This is guaranteed because we live in a sinful, fallen world. But resistance is good in that as we go through each trial, challenge, and obstacle, we become wiser, smarter, stronger, and more resilient when we encounter the next obstacle that will surely come our way.

PHYSICAL RESISTANCE

With physical fitness, muscles stretch and rip as a result of greater levels of resistance. As a result, those muscles adapt and grow when forced to work against that resistance. The benefits for those who work out are stronger bones, joints, and muscles, along with better balance. Mentally, working out physically increases independence, improves cognitive function, and reduces the risk of falls, especially for older adults.

MENTAL AND SPIRITUAL RESISTANCE

I pair mental and spiritual growth because they tend to go hand-in-hand. Adversity, challenge, and loss often lead us to spiritual questions regarding the existence of God or His presence and interaction in our life. These struggles build our inner fortitude (mental) alongside our faith (in God), resulting in spiritual and mental growth leading to character. Character is not built in the good times. In *The Problem of Pain*, C. S. Lewis wrote, "We can ignore even pleasure. But pain insists upon being attended to. God whispers to us in our pleasures, speaks in our conscience, but shouts in our pains: it is his megaphone to rouse a deaf world."[20]

The benefits of resistance in the mental and spiritual realm are increased perseverance, integrity, improved ability to handle stress, and stronger faith through a deeper reliance on God. The apostle Paul wrote, *Not only that, but we rejoice in our sufferings, knowing that suffering produces endurance, and endurance produces character, and character produces hope, and hope does not put us to shame, because God's love has been poured into our hearts through the Holy Spirit who has been given to us* (Romans 5:3–5).

In the end, resistance isn't only about physical strain; it's also about encountering challenges that force us to grow and adapt to the challenges we face not only in relation to our character in the present but also to achieve the greater things God has for us in the future. In other words, God allows resistance to help prepare us to live out His purpose for us with meaning and mission.

A WORLD FAILED FROM LACK OF RESISTENCE

A two-year experiment called Biosphere 2 was conducted in the 1990s. In it, scientists constructed a collection of sealed domes and greenhouses in the Arizona desert in an effort to recreate earth on a smaller scale. They created an artificial, self-contained environmental experiment on 1.27 hectare, or 3.13 miles vivarium, in the Arizona desert. The environment contained an 836-square meter ocean, complete with a coral reef, desert, grassland, and mangrove forest. Scientists expected to cultivate their own food and drink while maintaining breathable, livable levels of carbon dioxide and oxygen with as little help from outside the biosphere as possible.[21]

Biosphere 2 failed for several reasons, one of the main problems being the lack of resistance. In an article published by The University of Arizona titled "Biosphere 2," researchers noted that in the enclosed environment of Biosphere 2, trees grew rapidly but collapsed prematurely. The problem: The trees inside Biosphere 2 failed to reach maturity, collapsing under their own weight. The trees lacked the stress of wind, which causes trees to bend and sway and triggers the production of stress wood—a denser, stronger type of wood that helps trees withstand gravity and other stressors. This discovery highlighted the importance of environmental factors, like wind, in the development and resilience of trees, and by extension, other organisms.[22]

RESISTANCE GIVES LIFE COMPLETENESS

Resistance is part of life. While not always comfortable, it cannot be avoided if we want to grow strong and thrive. In *Man's Search for Meaning,* Holocaust survivor Viktor E. Frankl wrote about surviving three years in the Auschwitz and Dachau Nazi camps from 1942 to 1945. Speaking of his fellow prisoners, he said:

> *The way they bore their suffering was a genuine inner achievement. It is this spiritual freedom—which cannot be taken away—that makes life meaningful and purposeful. An active life serves the purpose of giving man the opportunity to realize values in creative work, while a passive life of enjoyment affords him the opportunity to obtain fulfillment in experiencing beauty, art, or nature. But there is also purpose in that life which is almost barren of both creation and enjoyment and which admits of but one possibility of high moral behavior: namely, in man's attitude to his existence, an existence restricted by external forces. A creative life and a life of enjoyment are banned to him. But not only creativeness and enjoyment are meaningful. If there is a meaning in life at all, then there must be a meaning in suffering. Suffering is an ineradicable part of life, even as fate and death. Without suffering and death human life cannot be complete.*[23]

Frankl went on to say,

> *The way in which a man accepts his fate and all the suffering it entails, the way in which he takes up his cross, gives him ample opportunity—even under the most difficult circumstances—to add a deeper meaning to his life. It may remain brave, dignified, and unselfish. Or in the bitter fight for self-preservation, he may forget his human dignity and become no more than an animal. Here lies the chance for a man either to make use of or to forgo the opportunities of attaining the moral values that a difficult situation may afford him. And this decides whether he is worthy of his sufferings or not. Do not think that these considerations are unworldly and too far removed from real life.*[24]

Going back to my family, the death and sickness we experienced so early in life was not a good thing in and of itself. But God used it for His good. He carried us through that time and converted our evil trials into good because we saw God's hand upon our family and trusted Him. First Peter 5:10 says, *And after you have suffered a little while, the God of all grace, who has called you to his eternal glory in Christ, will himself restore, confirm, strengthen, and establish you.* The key words there are *suffered a little while.*

RESISTANCE CAN LEAD TO GREAT BLESSINGS

My family is a beautiful story of God's grace, provision, love, protection, and blessing. It's also a testimony to our love for one another as a family. We suffered for a little while, and God took the resistance we faced and turned it into great blessings. While we didn't rejoice in our sufferings, we embraced them as a wall we prayerfully walked around, climbed over, or tunneled under, if need be. We acted with all our human strength, while depending on God's grace, power, and plan (mission) for our lives as He carried (and still carries) us through the impossible.

Two years after our family reunited, my Grandpa Sal, whom I loved, passed away. I was ten years old. My mother then contracted three additional minor cancers. As I write this in 2026, she is cancer free, and we are preparing to celebrate her ninetieth birthday. If you ask her about how she made it to ninety years old, she will tell you with great passion in Sicilian fashion (very directly) that it was "the hand of God and only the hand of God" on her that she survived to raise us.

On a secretary's salary, she raised us four children and financed our college years with no debt. Three of us went on to obtain a master's degree. My one brother who did not go to graduate school is just as, if not more, successful as he built a real-estate portfolio and runs a farm in Costa Rica, helping the less fortunate people in the mountains when he could be living in greater comfort by the beach. Each of us children married, stayed married, and went on to have children (and now grandchildren) of our own.

Each person experiences a unique life story. The result always boils down to depending on God to carry us through the resistance we encounter. Resistance is not a one-off event or a catastrophe. It's a regular part of life. God allows resistance in our lives to make us stronger, more resolved, and ultimately better prepared for the resistance still ahead. That is the necessity of resistance.

Whatever the circumstances, good or bad, through the peaks and valleys of life, God calls us to be content. But what does that mean? Are we to do nothing to move our purpose, meaning, and mission forward and just be content where we are, or are we to resist contentment in our current state because that kills creativity and success? This dilemma leads us to examine the quest for proper contentment in the next chapter.

4

THE QUEST FOR CONTENTMENT

The most outstanding characteristic of
Eastern civilization is to know contentment whereas that of
Western civilization is not to know contentment
–Hu Shih[25]

But godliness with contentment is great gain,
for we brought nothing into the world,
and we cannot take anything out of the world.
–1 Timothy 6:6–7

Years ago, I was asked to co-teach a course at my church called "Work for the Glory of God." The gentleman assigned to be my co-teacher was a very successful man who had started multiple successful companies over several decades. I met with my counterpart, and we laid out the full syllabus, which included a lesson on contentment. My counterpart asked me numerous times if he could teach that lesson and explained why he was passionate about the topic. His father, a machinist, was the most content man he had ever met—always joyful and full of life. In contrast, my counterpart said, even with all he had achieved and all the money he made, he had never obtained true contentment in the same way his father had.

I'm not certain if my friend ever discovered true contentment, but I submit that all too often the more we have, the more we want. And the more we want, the less content we are with what we have. I struggle with this too. Biblical wisdom literature, such as Proverbs and Ecclesiastes, provides the answer if we are ready to accept it. In America and the West in general, the greatest amount of wealth is spread among the fewest number of people, so as Christians, it is essential for us to examine the value of riches in our lives and in our family members' lives. I would assert that in our modern age, income discrepancies are a greater divider than cultural, racial, or ethnic differences. The only neutralizer is God and His Word. I pray that Christians and the church in general will worry less about building magnificent structures that consume tremendous amounts of money and resources and start using those blessings to execute their God-given purpose and mission in light of the Great Commission (Matthew 28:18–20).

FAMILIES WHO USE WEALTH WISELY

Many individuals and some entire families keep their wealth and success in a proper biblical perspective. In most cases, these people tend to donate a lot of money to good causes. And thank God for such people and families. A few examples include the Harrison family, the majority owners of Coca-Cola Consolidated; the Green family, owners of Hobby Lobby; and the Cathy family, owners of Chick-fil-A. These companies give away millions of dollars to help faith-based organizations achieve their God-given mission. And quite often, these organizations would not be able to achieve their goals without the generosity of such families. There are also smaller companies such as Walk in His Footsteps, a Christian faith-forward clothing and footwear company, that support charitable causes. But these companies are the exceptions to the rule. Too many individuals, organizations, and corporations are primarily focused on making and keeping the millions they make.

Money is neutral. God wants us to enjoy it, but He also desires that we use it as tool for His good. In fact, we can fully enjoy material things and recreation only if we view money for what it is and use it with a heart set on God's ways and Word. This is why I admire the families and companies I list in this chapter. They are an incredible source of encouragement and an example of what can be done.

John Davison Rockefeller (July 8, 1839–May 23, 1937) was an American industrial leader who played a pivotal role in the establishment of the oil industry and defended the modern structure of philanthropy. He was once asked, "How much money is enough money?" and he replied, "Just a little bit more."[26] This quote is often misunderstood and used to make a case against capitalism and making a profit. Nothing can be further from the truth. This conclusion is not only inaccurate but also depicts a distorted view of who Rockefeller was, what he was saying in that quote, and how he viewed his success and money. For example, in a 1905 interview he said, "God gave me my money. I believe the power to make money is a gift from God. ... I believe it is my duty to make money and still more money and to use the money I make for the good of my fellow man according to the dictates of my conscience."[27]

Most people overlook the fact that J. D. Rockefeller gave a lot of money away for the betterment of the community. And his family trust still does to this day. But how does that fit into his life purpose and mission? In another interview, he was asked about purpose in life and said that he also "believed strongly that his purpose in life was to make as much money as possible and then use it wisely to improve the lot of mankind."[28]

In a 2018 article published by Insider.com, Alison Millington wrote about sixty-two-year-old Lululemon Athletica Inc. founder Chip Wilson, who at that time was worth $3.9 billion according to Bloomberg. As the 496th richest person on the Bloomberg Billionaires index, Wilson was suffering from a rare form of muscular dystrophy and was spending $100 million on high-end treatments and research for a cure. As many flaws as Wilson may have had, he understood something about contentment. Speaking about the moment he found out he was a billionaire, in a 2016 interview he said, "There's not much difference between having probably $20 million and being a billionaire quite frankly."[29] Whether Millington was speaking of contentment in a way that most of us would or not, it's clear that in general, he could and would be content with being wealthy or super-wealthy. There is a big difference between many millions and billions, and I view his level of contentment as one that is noble for his situation.

PURPOSE, MEANING, MISSION, AND CONTENTMENT

What does contentment have to do with purpose, meaning, and mission? Everything. Purpose is what gives us meaning. And meaning defines our mission. If we get our purpose wrong, we misunderstand life's true meaning. And as a result, we get our mission wrong.

Years ago, I met a man at a Christian event who said to me, "Contentment is a curse word." He owned a business and made quite a bit of money, so his comment puzzled me. He then offered an explanation. When he was growing up, he said, his father was a fisherman and often gave fish to friends and those in need at no or low cost. The man's level of discontent and anger toward his generous father was obvious, so I asked him why it bothered him so much. He said his father was always a very happy person and loved the relationship he had with others, even though that detracted from his profit and the amount of money he could make. The father's generosity didn't affect the family's lifestyle, yet the son was annoyed by the fact that his father was content to live a simple life.

This man was very much an unscrupulous businessman in many ways, as he was strictly transactional and not relational in his business dealings. I concluded in the end that this young man very much misunderstood what contentment is. A false understanding of contentment can lead to laziness, for sure, but true contentment leads to peace, love, and spiritual richness, as we help others through a heart of kindness and generosity.

FINDING THE RIGHT BALANCE

In the United States, contentment can be understood two ways. The first is negative in that we are content in a society that allows for unlimited success, money, power, and notoriety. The second is positive regarding character, peacefulness, and understanding where God has placed us in life in the present moment. A problem often develops when people become too content and don't move far and hard enough in the direction of fulfilling their mission. We see this with people on government welfare, sometimes pensions, and even the wealthy with all their money, fame, power, and influence. Contentment is found in balancing hard work with commitment to family, marriage, friendships and health. We should never sacrifice what is truly important in the pursuit of what we might define as success.

Contentment in life and work is really about finding satisfaction and peace in what we do and what we have. If we think about it, isn't that in great part what the wealthy, the poor, and the middle class seek in life? Contentment is certainly not about settling for less in most cases. The one exception I believe might be the poor who seek to live on less through government money instead of working their way to a higher position to earn more money and live a life of meaning, purpose, and mission. It's not that the middle and very wealthy classes can't fall into this category but that more often than not, they don't.

Being content is a state of appreciating the present. It's about trusting that God is in control and that He is wise. We prioritize His will first and place our will and desires under His plan for our lives. Puritan Jeremiah Burroughs (1599–1646) said, "Christian contentment is that sweet, inward, quiet, gracious frame of spirit which freely submits to and delights in God's wise and fatherly disposal in every condition."[30] Burroughs' definition of contentment can be broken down into three parts. First, contentment is a mindset, one that is based on a humble spirit that understands contentment properly. Second, contentment is inward, in that it's learned. We must be disciplined in heart and mind in our quest for contentment as a heart work, digging deep into our mind, heart, and soul. Burroughs made clear that if it were as easy as keeping quiet outwardly, it would not require much learning. Third, contentment is quiet. In other words, it entails having a quiet heart and spirit as opposed to a tumultuous or angry spirit or mind. Burroughs no doubt read this Scripture passage: *But godliness with contentment is great gain, for we brought nothing into the world, and we cannot take anything out of the world. But if we have food and clothing, with these we will be content* (1 Timothy 6:6–8).

THE SECRET OF JOB CONTENTMENT

What about contentment in our career or vocation? This is one place we find a huge lack of contentment in American culture. In Man in the Mirror: Solving the 24 Problems Men Face, author and teacher Pat Morley wrote that according to a Gallup State of the American Workplace report, 70 percent of Americans don't find their work rewarding. Furthermore, in the pursuit of the material good life, most men don't find God's pleasure in their work. As a result, contentment becomes elusive and mysterious, as it was for my co-teacher friend mentioned earlier. Morley writes that nobody ever wins the rat race, because the rat race is unwinnable. The main stage for the rat race is the workplace, and men must feel a sense of accomplishment and satisfaction in their work or contentment will elude them.[31]

Morley went on to say that many men lack direction or don't understand God's will for their vocation, and he points to the fact that the book of Genesis makes clear that work is a blessing and not a curse. Genesis 2:15 says, *The Lord God took the man and put him in the garden of Eden to work it and keep it.* This was before the fall, so work was part of God's good plan for humanity. After Adam and Eve sinned, God cursed the ground and prescribed that *through painful toil you will eat food from it all the days of your life* (Genesis 3:17 NIV). Morely gives a powerful analogy in that the holiness of vocation is like or as close to the fabric of the Christian faith as the dye is to the cloth.[32]

Years ago, as Vice President of Operations for a search firm and job fair company out of the Washington DC area, I was called into a meeting with the national Vice President of Human Resources for Johnson and Johnson Company. We were conducting interviews, and he told me point-blank not to send him anyone who had been in the same job more than two years because that showed a lack of growth. His statement puzzled me. If God had created the person to be the best salesperson, why would the company want them promoted to be less effective as a sales manager? You cannot be the best salesperson in equal measure as a sales manager or in any other role.

We are all wired differently, and while growth is good, we ought not to punish people for being content in what they do for a living. When promotions or other changes are forced on someone who is gifted in a certain area, in most cases the person becomes less effective, less profitable, and less content. Why? Because they were created with a purpose. The role of salesperson is very different from that of a sales manager. Going to work every day with the wrong purpose erodes their sense of true meaning. As a result, their mission falters and eventually fails because it veers away from what God created them to be.

This is called the Peter Principle—the idea that competent employees are promoted until they reach a level where they are no longer competent. A top-performing salesperson, for example, has success; but having success in one role does not guarantee success in a higher, more demanding role that requires different skill sets. We were created with different skill sets, but no person has been or is gifted in every skill set. When we are promoted outside of our purpose, our mission ultimately suffers. Too often, this desire to move up is driven by our ego and lack of contentment with our position and pay level.

Morley went on to say that the secret of job contentment is *not* getting what you want. It's often contentment, or lack thereof, that challenges our desire to make more money, win prestige, gain respect, be more important, and increase status within our relationships. Are we content with our family, our spouse, and our marriage? The distinction between what we want (desire) and what we truly need has been a major point of discussion for all people throughout the ages. When we redefine what we want as something we need, we begin to become discontent.[33]

CONTENTMENT MISUNDERSTOOD

Understanding what something is can often be discovered by what that something is not. Contentment is no different. Contentment does not mean that you must sell all you have and move to a third-world country to serve God, unless the Lord calls you to such a mission. And most people are not called to such a mission. On the contrary, contentment entails surrendering your ambition and every other desire to Jesus Christ as a sacrifice to be used in fulfilling His plan for your life. This is what leads us to living with true purpose, meaning, and mission as opposed to missing God's great plan for our lives and lost blessings. When God calls us to purpose and mission, He gives us a heart desire for that specific purpose and mission. Even if you have never identified your calling, the Lord has a plan for your life. The difference between disregarding God's plan for your life and pursuing your own plan boils down to looking to God as the final authority in all areas of your life. In return you receive supernatural peace, fulfillment, and contentment despite the level of wealth God gives you.

Proverbs 11:24 says, *One gives freely, yet grows all the richer,* which means some are called to be wealthy while others are called to be less wealthy. It's a lot more difficult to live out the Christian faith as a wealthy person or family because the more wealth we have the more tempting it becomes to be self-dependent instead of God-dependent. I admire and respect people who have a great deal of wealth but remain humble and generous. I have concluded that if God wanted me to have more material wealth than I currently have, I would have more material wealth. If He wants me to have less, I will have less. I am grateful for all

He has given me, and I am happy He has not given me more based on my carnal desires. It all boils down to contentment. Benjamin Franklin said, "To be content makes a poor person rich, but to be malcontent makes a rich man poor."[34]

My friend who thinks that contentment is some kind of curse, by default disqualified himself from being content. My other friend, the co-teacher at church whose father was a simple machinist but the most contented man he has ever known, may never discover the best God has for his life. As far as I can tell, he has never been able to give up the golden ring of building companies and living on less wealth, even though he had more than enough money and resources to enjoy life materially speaking. This detrimental mindset has limited his ability to live out God's purpose and mission to the fullest. Such thinking, which many if not all of us struggle with to some extent, is simply holding off the inevitable of whatever comes next in life. We are to *commit to the Lord whatever you do, and he will establish your plans* (Proverbs 16:3 NIV), and through our contentment we will find peace in good times and in bad.

I have to pause and think about my level of contentment monthly, if not weekly, and sometimes daily in my pursuit of significance, purpose, and mission in order to keep doing what God has called me to do as opposed to what I have called myself to be and do.

CONTENT WHATEVER LIFE BRINGS

In closing, I leave you with the words of three of powerful, wealthy, and accomplished men regarding contentment. Toward the end of his life, John D. Rockefeller said, "I have made many millions, but they have brought me no happiness. I would barter them all for the days I sat on an office stool in Cleveland and counted myself rich on three dollars a week."[35] Rockefeller gave away millions of dollars over his lifetime.

Second, philanthropist Charles Fenney (1931–2023) was co-founder of Duty-Free Shoppers Group as well as Atlantic Philanthropies, one of the largest private charitable foundations in the world. While alive, Fenney gave away nearly his entire $8 billion fortune over many years, choosing to live modestly with his remaining wealth. He found purpose, meaning, and mission not in accumulating but in giving, proving that contentment comes from purpose not possessions, and from living simply not ostentatiously.

Third and last, let's close with one of the most accomplished, educated. and powerful men called by God in the New Testament Scriptures—the apostle Paul. In the book of Philippians, written while he was chained to a guard in a Roman prison, Paul wrote this: *Not that I am speaking of being in need, for I have learned, in whatever situation I am, to be content. I know how to be brought low, and I know how to abound. In any and every circumstance, I have learned the secret of facing plenty and hunger, abundance and need. I can do all things through him who strengthens me* (Philippians 4:11–13). So whether we start a business, take public office, become a machinist, or end up in prison because of our witness for Christ, contentment is key to fulfillment and meaning as we pursue God's purpose and mission for our life. In the next chapter, we begin to transition from our focus on purpose to working out our mission with meaning. Purpose gives us meaning in life.

5

FROM PURPOSE TO MEANING

In the realm of Nature there is nothing purposeless, trivial, or unnecessary.
—Maimonides[36]

When I was four or five years old, I wanted to be was a policeman. My Grandpa Salvatore DiMare, with whom I became very close after my father's passing, taught me that God sees everything and gives meaning to everything we do. He taught me that God is watching over us with His love and justice.

Why a policeman? A policeman is a peacemaker. The job carries a strong purpose and mission of maintaining a peaceful environment in our cities and keeping the bad guys off the street. This is a biblical value that Grandpa gifted me before I started kindergarten.

I learned this not only from what my grandpa said but also from how he lived. Through my grandpa's example, just as much was caught as taught. He taught me that connecting purpose to meaning involved everything I did in my daily life—like listening to what my mom said and being respectful and obedient to her. Meaning is about what we do with the deeper values and motivations God and our parents and grandparents instill in us. In other words, it's the *why* we do something. Meaning comes from feeling valued and connecting to something bigger through our purpose and mission. This comes from God through eternity, and eternity is something we cannot fully understand. Nevertheless, God places the mystery of eternity into the hearts of all men and women for a reason: to keep us seeking His truth, His Word, and His ways. And from this journey, meaning flows.

King Solomon said, *He [God] has made everything beautiful in its time. Also, he has put eternity into man's heart, yet so that he cannot find out what God has done from the beginning to the end* (Ecclesiastes 3:11). Solomon is telling us that God has given us an eternal perspective so we can look beyond the routine of life. Nevertheless, He has not revealed all of life's mysteries to us. God placed an eternal perspective and wonderment in our hearts as a deep-seated, compulsive drive to transcend our mortality by knowing the meaning and destiny of the world. Because we have been created in God's image (Genesis 1:27), we have an inborn inquisitiveness about eternal realities.

So how do we find meaning in life if all we see are micro moments of our own existence in the grand span of eternity? First, we accept that we are not in control of this world and that God has much more for us than we often seek ourselves. Ultimately, the answer lies within the Scriptures, which call people to live with meaning and a robust faith, even during times of trial and pain, because it is in our pain and suffering as much as in our accomplishments that meaning is most evident.

Let's turn our attention to the progression from purpose to meaning. The journey or movement from purpose to meaning starts with developing a basic understanding of our overarching life purpose and goals. An essential part of this development includes our experiences, which lead to a better understanding of the relationship between meaning and purpose (the *why* of life): Why am I here? What is my overall purpose? How does that purpose lead to meaning? As a result, coherence develops between the two (purpose and meaning) to the point of helping us better clarify our aspirations, goals, and mission. While purpose guides our future actions, meaning guides us in the present. And together they act as breadcrumbs in helping us make sense of the bigger picture of life purpose. Another thing that helps direct our purpose and meaning in life is identity.

IDENTITY: OUR COMPASS

Identity is how we see ourselves through the lens of our beliefs (religious or otherwise); it relates to our role in life (i.e. a mother, executive, etc.), and our affiliations with other people and organizations. Our identity helps provide continuity and meaning from childhood through adulthood. Identity is both internal and external—internal regarding the perception we have of ourselves and external in how we perceive what others think of us. Our identity acts as a personal compass that helps guide our decisions as well as connect with other people and God.[37]

Our identity, therefore, is a key component to discovering our purpose, meaning, and mission. If our identity is grounded in the Christian faith, the Bible is the road map for discovering purpose, meaning, and mission. If our identity is primarily linked to making money, then our values, meaning, and life mission become numbers-driven and money-focused. If our identity is connected to what other people think of us or expect of us, then we will likely never have a clear understanding of who we are or what our purpose, meaning, and mission are.

Our life purpose and meaning are formed in large part by our identity because our identity defines our core values along with our long-term goals and dreams. Through this process, our abstract goals turn into concrete daily actions and define our future life goals. Think of purpose as the compass and meaning as something formed through knowledge and life experiences. When those two are united, they navigate our purpose-driven compass and turn our abstract life goals into significance through actionable mission.

THE SEARCH FOR SIGNIFICANCE

When I was a young man, I was unaware and somewhat mixed up about life purpose hinging on significance as opposed to success. Cole A.

Randall said, "Success is all about what we do for ourselves; significance is all about what we do for others."[38] What we do for others comes out of our *selflessness* versus our *selfishness*. And our selflessness leads us to sacrifice for others when things seem helpless. In Portugal, I once spoke at a men's conference about evangelist Dwight L. Moody, who preached to over ten million people leading to over one million people becoming Christians. I then compared Dwight L. Moody to Edward Kimbal, who may have led only one person to the Christian faith. But that person was Dwight L. Moody. So, who led a more significant, purpose-driven, successful life? Moody or Kimbal? I would submit they were on par with each other. God gave Moody millions to speak to, while Kimbal was given one extremely important mission—to visit Moody at his job and speak to him about committing his life to Jesus Christ in the stock room of the shoe store Moody worked in.

It's up to God to elevate us—not ourselves. God determines the eternal significance of what we do. In today's world, we tend to place more value on the numbers than the souls—more value on what man finds significant and less on what God calls us to in living a life of significance and purpose. And this is where we tend to get turned around and misdirected.

SIGNIFICANCE AND PURPOSE

What is significance? For most of us, especially men, our significance and purpose revolve around our work. This is innately embedded in the way we were created from the very beginning when God took the man and put him in the garden of Eden to work it and keep it (Genesis 2:15). The challenge for you and me in our world and life is to ask ourselves, "Where am I considering seeking God's purpose for my life?"

When we speak of significance, we are reflecting on feeling valued in light of wanting what we do in this life to matter and be appreciated. In an article titled "Discover the 6 Human Needs," Tony Robbins writes that significance is one of the six most important needs and that it defines and drives our life-purpose.[39]

Significance, when properly understood and sought after leads to meaningful purpose. And man's search for meaning helps us answer the question of why we exist. Again, this is where we as humans in our social media, online, numbers-driven world often miss the mark. We often pursue significance and define our purpose through two basic portals. The first is through temporal, ego-driven goals such as fame, power, and material possessions. And the second is the desire to increase our reputation and notoriety. The problem with seeking significance, meaning, and life purpose through these things is that they often lead to doing immoral and sometimes illegal things in the name of achieving our self-defined and determined goals. Let's now turn our attention to purpose, considering the question, "What do I exist for?"

THE PURPOSE OF EXISTENCE

Why do we seek to live out a life of purpose to begin with? The answer in short is to have a positive influence on others, which gives the *why* for engaging in the mission or action of living out our life purpose. Famous atheist philosopher Friedrich Neitzsche said, "He who has a why to live can bear almost any how.[40] This idea is often connected to the work of psychiatrist Viktor Frankl whom I have written about in other chapters. Frankl developed *logotherapy,* a form of psychology designed to bring about healing through meaning. His approach is based on the belief that life has meaning under all circumstances, even suffering connected meaning to resilience in light of significance and purpose in life (see chapter 3).[41]

It's important to note that both companies and individuals serve others with a clear purpose. For example, as I mentioned in chapter 1, Coca-Cola Consolidated states publicly that their purpose to "honor God in all we do, to serve others, to pursue excellence, and to grow profitably."[42] Wouldn't it be wonderful if thousands of other companies in America and around the world had the same purpose? You and I can incorporate such values in our personal and corporate lives.

PUTTING PURPOSE INTO MOTION

A good starting point for turning purpose into action is the understanding that worse than success or failure is failing to live out your purpose in the first place. If paralyzed by fear of failure, we will never try anything or take any risks; consequently, we will miss our mission, calling, and purpose in life. In the movie *Braveheart*, William Wallace (played by Mel Gibson) is told by the girl who loves him that going into battle means he will die. She says, "You will die; it will be awful." Wallace responds, "Every man dies, but not every man really lives."

With that in mind, I want you to think of a time when you were called to do something in action with relation to your purpose in life. Was it scary or intimidating? It may have even been exciting. We as human beings want to achieve, excel, and conquer in our lifetime. The price of getting what you want without eternal purpose is more often than not a formula for disillusionment. Put another way, our life purpose disconnected from God is doomed to be less satisfying, more misleading, and limited to the temporal world. In other words, it has no eternal value. In the end, our failure to take some level of risk leads to failure to live out our life purpose, or at least to the degree or level God designed for us from eternity.

MAINTAINING PURPOSE AND SIGNIFICANCE

Why do we humans find it so difficult to take hold of such an identity of significance and purpose? First, we don't know our life purpose to begin with. Second, we often get frustrated and drop out of the race to seek our God-given purpose and meaning. This is true for people of all ages, both young and old. Third, for many of us, it's simply because we are confused between what we want from a worldly perspective and what the Bible defines as true meaning, purpose, and mission. Fourth, in some cases, we hit a ceiling, and we are not content in our present stage of life. Fifth, many of us think there must be more to life than "this"—wherever we are. With all these moving parts, the main thing is still life purpose.

In his bestselling book *The Purpose Driven Life*, Rick Warren writes, "The purpose of your life is far greater than your own personal fulfillment, your peace of mind, or even your happiness. It's far greater than your family, your career, or even your wildest dreams and ambitions. If you want to know why you're placed on this planet, you must begin with God. You were born by his purpose and for his purpose."[43]

Having a God-inspired vision for meaning and purpose is essential to your life, your family's lives, and your mission in the marketplace. Furthermore, a God-inspired purpose leads to becoming a value-added, morally reputable person or organization. It will set you apart. Identifying your life purpose will help you better understand why you get up every morning, and it will also lead to greater success in your mission. Discovering the why components change your priorities as purpose realigns your priorities. And when you keep your priorities straight, God will lead you to a compelling vision and purpose for your life, family, work, and business.

This is the importance of your quest for meaning and life purpose: God has prepared a unique role for you to play in this world, but it's up to you to discover that purpose and live it out through mission. Each one of us has a purpose and mission that will bring glory to God if we are faithful and obedient to that calling. Most of us at one time or another have asked ourselves what the meaning of life is and what our personal role in that existence is. As Rick Warren so eloquently said, it all starts with God. But what happens when life changes and our purpose seems to shift or change tracks?

WHAT'S NEXT?

In *From Purposeless to Purposeful*, friend and author Pastor Derwin Gray writes that after he retired from the NFL, he and his wife were faced with the daunting question of "What's next?" He says:

> *Who you are is vastly more important than what you do. And*

> *when you know who you are, you will be able to know what you are supposed to do. If you and I do not allow God to develop our identities, we will try to discover them through possessions, people, and popularity. This is like putting an expensive suit on a dead man. It's a funeral.*[44]

First, notice that Derwin is speaking about identity as we discussed earlier. Our identity plays a major part in defining our purpose. Derwin's identity is in Christ, and he is not wavering but excelling in God's purpose for his life. Derwin is saying that when our identity and character are shaped by Jesus, His thoughts, His character, and His actions then become ours. When you put God first, you discover all He has for your life purpose. God has numbered your days here on earth, and if you are faithful, He will fulfill every purpose He has planned for you. But keep in mind that your choices, thoughts, and actions affect how and to what extent your purpose and mission will be lived out. The progression from purpose to meaning to mission is developed throughout your life. This journey starts as you develop a basic understanding of your overarching life purpose and goals.

Personal growth and worldly success are often defined in terms of power, position, recognition, material possessions, and wealth. You want to keep these things in perspective in light of biblical principles. They are short-term achievements in our temporal world, and unless used rightly and to glorify God, they will eventually lead to an empty life. Worldly success, financial increase, and organizational growth are all wonderful achievements in proper context, but they should not come before your mission, anchored in godly principles. Failure to do so will take you off track into a purposeless, meaningless life direction. The *why* comes before what you do because the *why* is what defines your purpose. In the end, having a God-centered vision and purpose will expand your personal mission, growth, and eternal significance. This is how purpose leads to meaning.

6

WHAT IS MEANING?

The world is not divine sport; it is divine destiny.
There is divine meaning in the life of the world, of man,
of human persons, of you and me.[45]
–Martin Buber, *I and Thou* (1923)

Some might argue that meaning is subjective, but I disagree. Meaning flows from God; hence it cannot be subjective. Growing up, I was taught that whatever I do, do it right or don't do it at all. I understood that principle in the sense of avoiding the need to do the same thing twice, but I also realized that it implied that I should do everything with meaning, which may have involved pleasing my parents, employer, or friends (the *why*).

But what about God? Shouldn't the *why* for everything we do be to bring Him glory? After all, that is what He calls us to do. Jesus dying on the cross held great meaning for our lives on earth and our eternal salvation.

At an early age, I lived through the loss of a parent and also my other parent's nearly fatal cancer battle, which gave me an advantage when it comes to pondering the meaning of life. I was the kid who asked over and over, "Why, why, why?" Why did my father die when I was five years old? Why did my mother live when she was supposed to die of cancer three years after my father's death? I don't have the answer to either question, but I trust that God is in control and wants me to live life with faith and meaning.

Years ago, in my seminary Ethics class, Dr. Norman Geisler told us students that while we may know *that* something has occurred, we most often do not know *why* it occurred or occurred in the way it did. For many people, processing such a question entails too much brain power, emotional energy, and time. That takes us back to our earlier discussion about boredom. Failure to seek meaning in life carries the risk of developing a shallow faith.

Because God is infinite and His plans are beyond our comprehension, we never gain a complete understanding of our life's meaning, but we can still strive to live each day seeking the meaning (the *why*) He has for us that day. Our purpose changes throughout the seasons of life, and our meaning changes along with that changing purpose. We often find meaning in the monumental events, such as becoming a parent, but not in seemingly insignificant actions, like a good deed. But God sees meaning in the small and in the big. Consider this: Because there are many more small actions and events than big ones, God is most active in our everyday lives. That's why meaning is most often found in daily routines and events.

Let's now turn our attention to meaning. A good place to start is to address some differences between purpose and meaning. Understanding what something is not often helps us understand what that thing is. Purpose is like the reward at the end of a race. We work hard for things yet to come and run fast to win the race. As such, meaning naturally connects to action in the form of life mission. (We'll get to mission in greater detail in a later chapter.) For now, let's simply say that meaning is more about understanding the past in light of what we want to accomplish in the future. Meaning is about understanding the why behind the things we do and think. It's about defining our significance and where that comes from as well as defining what we consider to be of value—a key component of why we do anything. Value in application leads us to pursue what is important, valuable, and useful to our life mission. That something can be personal, relational, or even monetary. It's wise to examine all things we consider to be of value and ask ourselves why we consider those things valuable before committing them to life purpose.

PURPOSE: FOR EVIL OR FOR GOOD?

Purpose not only helps us define life meaning but also creates it. When disconnected from God, one's purpose can be bad and evil. For example, the well-known conservative speaker Charlie Kirk was murdered by a man who had an evil purpose. What this young man saw as his purpose in life was to take another person's innocent life for selfish, evil reasons. Kirk's alleged killer is a twenty-two-year-old Utah man named Tyler Robinson. His life meaning became entangled with Antifa and radical hatred against conservative values and those who successfully communicated them. Robinson is a former straight-A student from a good family, whose parents and siblings love him. Sadly, he turned so radically evil that his purpose and self-proclaimed life meaning led him to turn against God, family, and Charlie Kirk. In some distorted way, Robinson thought that murdering Charlie Kirk was good because Robinson decided that what Kirk stood for—which was the truth and God—was evil. As a result, Robinson thought and acted in ways completely opposite of what is truly good.

Consider the young man Jesus spoke about in the book of Mark:

> *And as he [Jesus] was setting out on his journey, a man ran up and knelt before him and asked him, "Good Teacher, what must I do to inherit eternal life?" And Jesus said to him, "Why do you call me good? No one is good except God alone. You know the commandments: "Do not murder, Do not commit adultery, Do not steal, Do not bear false witness, Do not defraud, Honor your father and mother."* (Mark 10:17–19)

Robinson broke several commandments: he *murdered* Charlie Kirk, *stole* the husband and the father of Charlie's wife and children, then *lied* in attempt to elude the law. He also *defrauded* his family so badly that his father turned him into the police. Robinson failed at living a life of good purpose and meaning, which resulted in a horrible mission.

On the contrary, we find people such as Billy Graham, Mother Theresa, and yes, Charlie Kirk. Charlie Kirk, like Billy Graham and Mother Theresa, dedicated his life to helping others. In Kirk's case, he respectfully but directly debated people in love and in truth. Kirk's purpose was to influence college students to help them see all things in truth, based on logic, and grounded in the Christian faith for eternal reasons. But Kirk was also very respectful to all the people he interacted with and to all religions, including Mormonism, which he complimented minutes before being assassinated. Remember, meaning naturally leads to action in the form of life mission. What we saw on the outside was Charlie Kirk's mission. He found meaning through his understanding of the past, which instructed his actions in the present for the future. What was that future? Raising up truthful, conservative, loving people and leaders equipped to revive American culture and the world for God's goodness. So it makes sense that Kirk's purpose, meaning, and mission were based on Christian values.

Purpose to meaning to mission cuts both ways, though, so we must be careful as to how we order our daily lives—what we put into our minds—because that ultimately influences and eventually defines our mission. If you are wondering what is the best thing any of us can do, it's seeking God through biblical study and prayer. God and only God is good, and He will supernaturally guide us in and through His goodness. The *why* behind our meaning directs our next steps to living meaningfully.

LIVING A MEANINGFUL LIFE

Most people seek meaning in life. Some of us seek meaning through good means and others through bad means. Remember, meaning simply reflects things that mean something to you. This can encompass family values, work ethic, financial riches, ego, power, the desire to help others, or even please God. In the end, meaning directs our mission.

Some years ago, I met a Christian who had relocated from Massachusetts to Charlotte, North Carolina, in search of a better life. Up north, he operated a small convenience store that sold liquor and tobacco products. He eventually concluded that running such a business wasn't adding value and didn't reflect God's goodness. In some cases he was hurting people by selling liquor and tobacco products to them. As a result, he sold his business to seek another way to provide for his family.

In contrast, my friend in the Washington DC area owns a home health care business. Through that business he helps older people live a more comfortable life, and in some cases live longer in better health. My friend finds purpose in caring for others and finds meaning in helping those older people and their families live more comfortable, less stressful, healthy lives. His home health care business is based on the Christian values of authentically caring for people and putting people above profit. He lives a life of deep meaning.

Before we move on, let's look at the second part of meaning in mission, which comes down to making money. We all need to make money, and money is good until we love it more than we love God and others. A good question to periodically ask ourselves is "What will I have to sacrifice to make that (additional) money, and what will I do with the money I make?" Overwhelmingly, most people do not handle great sums of money very well, including most Christians. The Bible says, *For the love of money is a root of all kinds of evils. It is through this craving that some have wandered away from the faith and pierced themselves with many pangs* (1 Timothy 6:10).

Most people misunderstand and misquote 1 Timothy 6:10 by saying it this way: *Money is the root of all evil.* But money is not the root of all evil; the verse says that *the love* of money is *a root of all kinds of evil.* It takes money to run a home health care business, take a vacation, eat dinner, and finance your kids' education. Those are good uses of money. The problem surfaces when we begin to love money, which becomes the root of all kinds of evil, not all evil. *Love of money* and *all kinds of evil* are the key phrases.

Some people manage their money as a resource and don't *love it* at its core. These rarities are role models for all of us. Let's look at some of them, starting with the owners of the privately owned retail chain specializing in arts, crafts, and home décor—Hobby Lobby.

Hobby Lobby founder David Green explains that the company gives 50 percent of their profits away each year. In an interview with Fox News's Laura Carrione titled, "Hobby Lobby Founder Explains Decision to 'Give Away Ownership' of Company: 'Joy in Giving What We Have,'" this is what Green said:

> *"We really wanted to do something that mattered a hundred years from now. Instead of just absorbing things ourselves, we wanted to do things in various ministries," Green told host Stuart Varney. "We do something real novel: you get what you earn. If you don't earn anything, you don't get anything. … But no one actually creates a lot of wealth," the CEO said of his Christian-owned company's structure. "Wealth can be a curse; we all do well, working in the company and get[ting] paid for what we do. So we see ourselves as, really, stewardships of the profits that we earn." On Monday, Varney asked Green if customers can expect Hobby Lobby, with its 969 arts-and-crafts stores in 47 states, to fund Christianity and ministries across the country—to which the founder replied with an emphatic "yes."*[46]

Green has connected life purpose to meaning and mission. He admits that they wanted to do "something that mattered." They have purpose, which has in turn motivated them to do something of meaning for both the present and the future. Remember, meaning is more about understanding the *why* behind the things we do and think. It is about defining our significance and knowing where that comes from. Green has created a clear, long-term, meaningful legacy full of purpose and mission that is selfless. His vision is for his work to make money and then to give half of it to help other nonprofits in their mission. And as he stated, he wants mission to continue going "a hundred years from now." Think about that—he won't be alive a hundred years from now, but his legacy will. When we live only looking at the present, we live selfishly. This in turn materializes in a selfish mission based on short-term gain. And short-term gain more often than not leads to chaos in life because materialism doesn't satisfy the heart, soul, or mind.

THE SEARCH FOR TEMPORAL MEANING

Many people seek a meaningful life through human desires, material things, pleasure, and many other secular ways. Dr. Jordan Peterson comments on this in *12 Rules for Life: An Antidote to Chaos.* To have meaning in your life is better than to have what you want, he says, because you may neither know what you want nor what you truly need. He argues that meaning is something that simply comes upon you of its own accord. You can set up the preconditions for it and follow meaning when it manifests itself in life, but you cannot simply produce it as an act of the will.[47]

I agree with Peterson to a certain extent in that, yes, we can set up preconditions for meaning in life, but God is behind all of this, giving everything we do an ultimate value and meaning to begin with. I agree that we can't produce meaning, but we certainly can strive to live a life focused on what is good. The best example I've had of living a life of meaning is my mother. Her name is Vita, which means "life" in Italian. Even in her older years, she is full of love and life. She has taught me firsthand that to live a life of meaning is to truly be alive, and to truly be alive in light of God's hand upon our life is to live a life full of true meaning. That's a decision we make at the start of each day.

MAKE EACH DAY MEANINGFUL

Where do we start? A good beginning for each day is to wake up and thank God for another opportunity to fill another meaningful day. Start each day with a desire to extract and achieve the most amount of meaning in it. One way to accomplish that is by creating and carrying out a to-do list at the beginning of the day. I am a big proponent of to-do lists. I usually write out my to-do lists at the end of the day for the following day by thinking about what I need to do and what I would like to accomplish the following day. Doing this helps me make each day more productive and meaningful.

At the end of the day, as you prepare to go to sleep, review that day's events. Try to identify how you used the opportunities you were afforded and how you fulfilled those opportunities in relation to your life purpose. Then, before you close your eyes, resolve within your soul to make the next day even more meaningful regarding fulfilling all that lies ahead. By doing so, you will instill new meaning into every activity that falls between waking up and going to bed every day.

MEANING IN DAILY PRACTICE

When you eat, you're not only satisfying your hunger; you're also giving your body and soul the nourishment it needs to help you live out your meaning for that day. The same is true of your work life. When you conduct business, you aren't just surviving; you're using your skills and talents to help refine the world by acting rightly, conducting business ethically, and teaching others through virtuous examples. Sleep is our opportunity to rest our physical bodies and minds, which in turn rejuvenates our souls. Returning our mind, body, and soul to a place of rest and rejuvenation, detached from our material worries, refreshes our soul so it's ready to enter the next day in a new meaningful way.[48]

MEANING IN DYING

Living with meaning necessitates a healthy understanding of dying. The one thing in our future that is certain is death, and we are wise, when we go to a funeral, to allow the coffin to inform us of our journey's end before we get there. That may sound morbid, but try this the next time you are at a funeral. Stop at the casket and stare into the coffin at the person for two to ten minutes, allowing the past to inform your future.

You will be looking at what represents the termination point of the entire physical lifetime of that person here on earth. Ask yourself to summarize what went on during the dash of their lifetime—between their birth and death dates.

From death, life emerges in eternity. Jordan Peterson says this about death, eternity, and meaning:

> *It's meaning that emerges beautifully and profoundly like a newly formed rosebud opening itself out of nothingness into the light of sun and God. ... Meaning happens when that dance has become so intense that all the horrors of the past, all the terrible struggle engaged in by all of life and all of humanity to that moment becomes a necessary and worthwhile part of the increasing successful attempt to build something truly Mighty and Good.*[49]

Meaning must have an eternal end or goal which works backward from the past toward the present. This builds year by year, month by month, week by week, day by day, and moment by moment.

It is meaning that dictates how we live out our mission(s) in life. And there are good missions and bad ones. The good ones are birthed out of meaning which comes from God.

What is the meaning you seek as a person? Better yet, how can you identify meaning in life and live out that meaning through mission? Examining this question is essential because without meaning, there is no purpose, and without purpose there is no mission. And without mission, we live a directionless life, becoming idle agents responsible for wasted opportunities. As a result, we miss the best God has for us and our ability to affect others for the better. If you go too long without life meaning, you will end up seeking things you think might fill that void.

I learn a lot about meaning through my children. My son wants to build a business one day; his twin, my first daughter, wants to become an architect. My youngest daughter wants to rebuild people's mouths through dental work. I think she is going to build something out of this world; something we cannot yet imagine. People find meaning in building things for the simple reason that God is the Ultimate Creator and Designer of the universe, and we are created in His image. We build farms, factories, families, governments, swimming pools, hospitals, and the list goes on. In the end, we are God's legacy, as the only creatures made in His image. And that infuses our lives with incredible meaning.

7

UNPREDICTABLE SUCCESS

Success or failure cannot be measured by any human standard.[50]

Purpose and meaning are often confused with success. True success often involves aligning one's action with internal values rather than external validation. Society often imposes meaning and definitions of success that cause individuals to lose touch with their personal life goals and objectives. Understanding the differences starts with moving from a mindset of chasing outcomes to finding meaning in the journey itself. The conduit to successfully bridging purpose to success is our pursuit of significance.[51] And the correct way of understanding success in light of purpose is to seek and value significance over and above success. This entails shifting one's focus from simply achieving status to creating good, lasting value. This is often referred to as moving from "success to significance."

When I lived in the Washington DC area, a common saying was, "It's not what you know but who you know." When opportunities arose, they usually boiled down to who you knew and timing—being in the right place at the right time. I worked for a computer company called Compucom, selling computer hardware and software solutions to U. S. federal government agencies. On one occasion in the early 1990s, I was bidding on a contract for thousands of computer chips. I brought in my manager, who helped me craft a competitive proposal offer. I lost a bid worth many thousands of dollars because my bid came in ten dollars over the top competitor's. I am more than confident the bid was decided under the table, and I was allowed to bid as a check price, which is intended to keep the other party honest in their pricing. I was very disappointed, but my manager chuckled and said, "You win some and lose some."

About a week later, I received a call from a contact I had never met at a government agency that was my account. He asked if we carried HP Super Computers on GSA (government approved list). We did, and he bought two of them for over $20,000 each. That was a lot of money for two servers at that time. I learned a good lesson that day. The victory is not always to the smartest or the wisest or the most athletic, skilled, or even prepared. To a great degree, time and chance play a role in our success. When we look at others as more successful than ourselves, we tend to see them as having more purpose and meaning. But such thinking is not correct. Time and chance play a significant role even in the lives of most famous people, and if not careful, we will view our purpose and meaning as trivial when compared to others who are more successful on the surface, secular level.

How many artists become famous and how many remain undiscovered? The answer is that many great artists are undiscovered. Why? Because defining *best* is often subjective and may have very little to do with an objective set of criteria rewarding those competing for the top spot(s). In a 2024 article published by hypebot.com, writer Bobby Owsinski notes that 87.6 percent of all musicians releasing music are "undiscovered." He says,

> *Now it's important to understand that "making it" means different things to different people. Some musicians are perfectly happy just making a living playing music, while others have a drive to get their music out to as many people as possible. "Making it" is different in both cases. That said, if you have dreams of becoming a music*

> *superstar, don't expect going viral on Tik Tok or Instagram to do it for you. The odds are really stacked against you."* [52]

Simply put, success in great part depends on time and chance.

CHANCE, LUCK, AND TIMING

What is the key to success? In this chapter, I am going to show you that success in life is unpredictable and why one's ability and intelligence are no guarantee for success in one's life or in the marketplace.

In an article titled "Luck and Timing: Crucial for Success?" Katarina Åhlin, CFR Global Executive at Search Sweden, answers that question as follows:

> *What makes some people have successful careers with prestigious titles at the most exciting companies? If you ask individuals who hold these positions, it is not uncommon to hear answers like "talented," "worked harder than others," "sacrificed a lot," "extremely ambitious," and "had a clear plan." While these factors may be true—wholly or partially—they probably don't tell the whole truth. We dare to claim that both luck and timing can play a significant role in determining who reaches the highest leadership positions and who falls short."* [53]

Why does chance play a major role when it comes to success? In an entry on QUORA, Peter Ho, a former software engineer at Google, writes this response to that question: "It [chance or timing] plays a large role in life. Success is mostly about managing chance. The rich like to downplay the role of chance in order to make them look good." [54]

WHAT THE ANCIENTS SAY

Biblical scriptures are the most widely read source for wisdom and knowledge in history. So what does the Bible say about timing and chance in relation to success? Is chance the same as luck? Is chance part of God's plan? To answer those questions, let's look at Ecclesiastes 9:11. This verse makes clear that the richest people are not the most intelligent and that the battle is not necessarily won by the strongest people or militaries; neither are influence and power necessarily held by those who have favor. On the contrary, King Solomon, author of Ecclesiastes, tells us quite the opposite. He wrote, *But time and chance happen to them all.* Zooming out, the verse fits into a larger passage which says:

> *Again, I saw that under the sun the race is not to the swift, nor the battle to the strong, nor bread to the wise, nor riches to the intelligent, nor favor to those with favor, but time and chance happen to them all. (Ecclesiastes 9:11)*

SUCCESS AND INTELLIGENCE

Most people consider themselves smarter than other people in one way or another. In truth, God is the smartest being ever to exist. How is He the smartest being in existence? First, He is omniscient. This means He knows all things or holds all knowledge. There is nothing God does not know. Second, God is eternal, meaning that He has neither past nor future, but simply IS. In His essence, He can only be I AM. *"God said to Moses, I AM WHO I AM* (Exodus 3:14). Only God is pure actuality. He has no potentiality. You and I as human beings have both actuality (we exist) and potentiality (not to exist). God is a necessary being as the Eternal-Uncreated-Creator. Combine His omniscience with His eternality and the product is eternal knowledge.

God is in full control of all things, but that does not mean He makes all things happen with or without our effort or agreement—including our success. In His great eternal plan, He uses timing, circumstances, events, jobs, opportunities, and even catastrophes to purify and guide life's events. He uses those same things to propel us, refine us, and reward us in light of our success. Some Christians, after being rewarded with worldly blessings (wealth, authority, influence, etc.), sadly lose their way and use their blessings for selfish gain and/or other immoral reasons. Why does God allow such behavior? The answer is that He allows us free will.

I was privileged to grow up and live in the Washington DC area for thirty-four years. My father was an electrical engineer for the federal government at the Department of the Navy in downtown Washington, D.C. Did I choose to be in the right city, at the right time, with the right people? Or was it time, chance, and God's providence?

People still come from all over the country to work in the Washington D.C. area. So why are some people able to enter such a great situation in this powerful city while others aren't? The answer is simple. To some degree, each person must have a college degree, know someone to get a job, and be prepared on multiple levels. Each person must be ready to jump on an opportunity and be available and willing to accept the opportunity for success at the exact moment it presents itself. A lot of success in Washington, DC, and many other places boils down to "being in the right place at the right time and knowing the right people." Contrary to popular belief, it's a lot more about who you know than what you know. Timing and chance.

A TIME FOR EVERYTHING

King Solomon wrote that there is a *time for everything* in Ecclesiastes 3:1–8. If we are not operating within God's timing, we will most likely have false expectations, so we are wise to seek God's true path for success for our life at that specific time in history according to His plan. Solomon wrote,

> *For everything there is a season, and a time for every matter under heaven: a time to be born, and a time to die; a time to plant, and a time to pluck up what is planted; a time to kill, and a time to heal; a time to break down, and a time to build up; a time to weep, and a time to laugh; a time to mourn, and a time to dance; a time to cast away stones, and a time to gather stones together; a time to embrace, and a time to refrain from embracing; a time to seek, and a time to lose; a time to keep, and a time to cast away; a time to tear, and a time to sew; a time to keep silence, and a time to speak;*

a time to love, and a time to hate; a time for war, and a time for peace. (Ecclesiastes 3:1–8)

THE BOTTOM LINE WITH SUCCESS

Think about how many artists, government workers, business people, and others became famous or successful. How many people in all professions are undiscovered? As I said earlier, most people remain relatively unknown. Why? Time and chance.

Life is unpredictable and so is our success in many cases. This is why our ability is no guarantee of success. Similarly, death is also unpredictable. Solomon wrote, *For man does not know his time. Like fish that are taken in an evil net, and like birds that are caught in a snare, so the children of man are snared at an evil time, when it suddenly falls upon them* (Ecclesiastes 9:12). What we can do is pray for God's wisdom, direction, and will for us at each major turn. After that, the best path to success is to place ourselves in the right place at the right time. This entails a combination of preparation, awareness, and seizing opportunities when they present themselves as opposed to intentional positioning and creating our own opportunities. All of this combined with seeking God's will is the secret sauce in unpredictable success.

When purpose and meaning are confused with success, we tend to confuse success with life purpose. So, it's wise to evaluate our vocation, career, and life mission from the perspective of aligning our actions with our internal values based on our purpose and what we find meaningful rather than from external validation only. Psalm 37:4 says, *Delight yourself in the Lord, and He will give you the desires of your heart.* When we seek His will and purpose, our desires, purpose, and meaning become His. Success becomes sustainable when driven by our purpose. When we integrate what we consider meaningful with our core values and apply that to our professional goals, we begin to create a unique clarity for our overall purpose.

It's important to note that we must constantly evaluate where we are at by asking *why* in order to ensure that our actional mission remains aligned with our evolving life mission and that of the organization we run or work at. When our life work of stay-at-home mom, manager, entrepreneur, or whatever we choose is more than a job, our contribution reaches a whole new level, leaving a positive, lasting mark on the world as our legacy. (We will discuss legacy later in the book.)

Understanding the differences between purpose and success is essential. Confusing the two can and will take you off track from living out your true purpose to the fullest degree. A good way of understanding success in light of purpose is to view and value significance over and above success. This entails shifting one's focus from simply achieving status to creating good, lasting value. This is important, so let's go one step further to look more closely at our pursuit of success. From there, we can work backward from how we might view success and obtain a long-lasting, purpose-driven mission. The more we strive for success without true, authentic purpose, the more we miss our God-given purpose. And the pursuit of success without purpose and meaning will be a futile endeavor.

8

THE PURSUIT OF SUCCESS

Success or failure cannot be measured by any human standard.[55]

In 1995, Bob Buford wrote the bestselling book *Halftime*, which popularized the concept of "moving from success to significance" in the second half of life. Buford realized that many people work their entire lives to achieve material success only to find they lack happiness and a sense of purpose when that success finally comes. And he rightly encouraged people to seek out meaning and impact in their later years.[56] I believe that finding material or earthly success is not difficult if you apply yourself. But if not careful, finding success can easily lead to the loss of purpose. What good is success if it results in internal emptiness despite all of your external achievements? I have heard countless stories of individuals who lost everything, only to rediscover their true purpose and calling when their life crashed. Let's try not to be that person. In this chapter, we will examine what success is and evaluate our individual achievements within the context of our desire to discover real purpose, meaning, and mission.

Austrian psychiatrist and Holocaust survivor Viktor E. Frankl said,

> *Don't aim at success—the more you aim at it and make it a target, the more you are going to miss it. For success, like happiness, cannot*

> *be pursued; it must ensue, and it only does so as the unintended side-effect of one's dedication to a cause greater than oneself or as the by-product of one's surrender to a person other than oneself. Happiness must happen, and the same holds for success: you must let it happen. Happiness must happen by not caring about it. I want you to listen to what your conscience commands you to do and go on to carry it out to the best of your knowledge. Then you will live to see that in the long run—in the long run, I say!—success will follow you precisely because you had forgotten to think of it.*[57]

THE FUTILE PURSUIT OF SUCCESS

Let's break down what Frankl said regarding true success. First, it "cannot be pursued." When we pursue success in and of itself, more often than not, we end up pursuing the material things of this world—namely, wealth, fame, power, and fortune. None of these things in and of themselves equate to success or happiness. What we do with these things goes on to define our success.

Second, success is not something that naturally ensues from our effort; it is an "unintended side-effect" of one's dedication to a mission, which Frankl calls a "cause greater than oneself." In other words, success is a derivative of our actions not simply what we do with our talents and resources.

Third, Frankl said that success is obtained as an unintended side-effect of one's dedication to a "cause greater than oneself or as the by-product of one's surrender to a person other than oneself." I would submit that the person or cause referred to here is more often than not God. The only other option or cause would be self, meaning that we place ourselves first in our ambitions, talents, and mission. I believe that focusing so intensely on the self is what leads to failure and misery for many people in that they seek their own pleasure and happiness instead of executing their true calling and mission in life—the ones designed for them by God.

Finally, Frankl gives us the secret behind obtaining success in the last line cited above, in decrying that success will follow you precisely because you have not made it the central goal of your life's desire. As a trained psychologist who survived a Nazi prison camp as a Jewish prisoner and as a man who pursued God throughout his life, Frankl ended up bumping into the truth about how to obtain real success.

GOALS, CARREER, AND SUCCESS

Jordan Peterson said in a Fox News interview that "happiness is when you are progressing toward a (value added) goal, toward something that's a 'value goal.' No goal—won't be happy." [58] A professional career, including raising children as a career, is how people most often define their life success. So, what is the value of a career? Is it to make a life or a living? Is there value in climbing the proverbial ladder of success? Does climbing it equate to true success?

In a LinkedIn article titled, "The Meaning of Success and How to Define Success in Life," Eugene Adu-Wusu defined success as follows:

> *Success (the opposite of failure) is the status of having achieved and accomplished an aim or objective. Being successful means the achievement of desired visions and planned goals. Furthermore, success can be a certain social status that describes a prosperous person that could also have gained fame for its favorable outcome. The dictionary describes success as the following: "attaining wealth, prosperity and/or fame."* [59]

Adu-Wusu then pointed out that the only person who can define your success in life is you. He was wise to point out that some define success in terms of prosperity—i.e. luxurious cars and a huge mansion—while others define success in terms of freedom or a life full of joy and happiness with their family.

As I read his article, I concluded that material success is limited in scope but does have value, while success found in God, family, friends, and a well-balanced life personifies the joy found in material success and the things in life. Furthermore, Adu-Wusu differentiated between accomplishments and success. Accomplishments are the result(s) we desire based on expected, attempts to reach a specific goal(s). Success, on the other hand, is the positive consequence or outcome of that accomplishment. In order to achieve our accomplishments and success, we must have goals. Achieving our goals can be good or bad depending on how much we are willing to sacrifice and who or what we are willing to sacrifice to achieve them.[60]

In *Free to Succeed*, author Steve Diggs wrote that our society equates success with money, power, and sexual conquests. I agree, and nothing much has changed since that book's publication in the 1990s, except that this exact definition of success has been increasingly implemented by the U.S. and the global world order. Diggs wrote that after the death of a famous Hollywood star, columnist Rona Barrett was asked if she knew of any other superstar in the world of entertainment or sports that might be in danger of taking their lives. Her answer was shocking in that she didn't know of any superstars who were not in danger of either deliberately or accidentally taking their own lives due to their unhappiness. In spite of having everything under the sun in terms of material goods, true happiness eludes people of all classes, even the most wealthy, famous, and powerful people. This leads us to conclude that there has to be much more to success than fame, prosperity, money, power, and sex.[61]

TWO ESSENTIAL INGREDIENTS

King Solomon, the richest man to ever live according to his era's economy, said this: *Then I considered all that my hands had done and the toil I had expended in doing it, and behold, all was vanity and a striving after wind, and there was nothing to be gained under the sun* (Ecclesiastes 2:11). In spite of his wealth, wisdom, and accomplishments, Solomon concluded that success in and of itself is empty and meaningless. Why? That recipe for success lacks two crucial ingredients.

The first ingredient of true success is realizing that it starts with accepting the fact that God wants us to enjoy real happiness and success. What God considers to be success in our lives is usually different from what we consider success. As sinful human beings, we are told to push hard and promote ourselves all the way to the top of the most downloaded list, the best-seller list, or the most watched YouTube channel. On the other hand, Jesus tells us that success comes when we do not strive to be the most famous, the wealthiest, or the most prominent person in the room. In Luke chapter 14, Jesus makes clear that we are to pursue the mission God calls us to do out of joy, love, and obedience. In that process, God will raise us up: *Humble yourselves before the Lord, and he will lift you up* (James 4:10).

Here's what Jesus says in Luke 14:

> *Now he told a parable to those who were invited, when he noticed how they chose the places of honor, saying to them, "When you are invited by someone to a wedding feast, do not sit down in a place of honor, lest someone more distinguished than you be invited by him, and he who invited you both will come and say to you, "Give your place to this person," and then you will begin with shame to take the lowest place. But when you are invited, go and sit in the lowest place, so that when your host comes he may say to you, "Friend, move up higher." Then you will be honored in the presence of all who sit at table with you. For everyone who exalts himself will be humbled, and he who humbles himself will be exalted."* (vv. 7–11)

I believe that when we get to heaven, God is going to look favorably on those who humbly served others considering the talents—meaning the platform, audience and opportunities—God gave them. Some famous Christians may be surprised that their self-promoted high levels of success were not credited to their heavenly account due to their self-serving motives. *That* we do something ought to follow *why* we do that something. For those who want to be morally in line with biblical values, that desire ought to be bathed in prayer and humble servanthood. That may sound very old school and out of touch with our present self-serving world, but it's the biblical truth.

The second ingredient of success lies in our teachability, that is our learning to listen when God guides us. How does He guide us? Through His Word and through the Holy Spirit, who gives us wisdom and principled direction. In Psalm 119:105, the psalmist writes, *Your word is a lamp to my feet and a light to my path.* And Jesus promised His disciples, *"When the Spirit of truth comes, he will guide you into all the truth"* (John 16:13). God may also use godly friends, family members, and ethical marketplace leaders. God can and does speak to us through other people, but we must be careful to run what others say through the Word of God so as not to be misled by another sinful person with an ulterior motive or a misunderstanding of the situation or truth.[62]

PURSUE A GREATER CAUSE

Let's remember what Viktor E. Frankl said in that we are not to aim at success as a target but rather pursue a greater cause and success will follow naturally. If we base success on a dollar amount, we will not only be disappointed, but we will also hurt others as well as ourselves along the way to getting rich, famous, and successful. We must allow success to happen in God's time according to His will, timing, and plan. If we are humble and realistic about what success truly is, we won't be disappointed. And in the long run, success will follow.[63]

9

WHAT IS MISSION?

What I really lack is to be clear in my mind what I am to do, not what I am to know. ... The thing is to understand myself to see what God really wishes me to do ... to find the idea for which I can live and die.[64]
–Søren Kierkegaard

When I reached my middle-age years, like most people, I began to think about time differently, focusing more on the eternal than the temporal. The older we grow, the more often we face the deaths of those we love— friends, neighbors, and co-workers. I have always wanted to live out the latter part of my life serving God and others, but when those latter years arrived, I realized that it's "now or never."

What did God intend for my life from an eternal perspective? I looked around at many of my friends who have a vast amount of wealth but lack a substantive life purpose, meaning, and mission. Remember that mission is a verb. It's not enough to feel like we're doing something significant; we must do something significant. This cemented my resolve to move toward a full-time commitment in my nonprofit work and less time in my corporate job. With age came a newly discovered resolve. And with that resolve comes something even scarier—dependence on others. We all need to eat. The more money we have in the bank, the freer we are when it comes to living out our life mission, or so conventional thinking would have us believe. But in most cases, life doesn't work that way.

What usually happens is that we get more tired with age. We've worked hard, so it's time to relax and take it easy. The problem is that mindset can take away or eliminate our ability to live out our mission. One man whom I worked with for ten years before the corporate office bought him out said that he was going to retire, move to Florida, and play tennis. Within twenty-four months, he had a fatal heart attack. When alive, he was instrumental in helping me feed my family and live out my mission through my not-for-profit ministry. The point is that we often think we will live forever or that we somehow deserve to take it easy and do nothing that is missional. Nothing can be further from the truth.

I got to know a gentleman at the YMCA. He and his family were from the Washington DC area, as I was. His parents worked for the federal government as mine did. He was Jamaican, and his political affiliation was the opposite of mine, but we were friends because we respected each other and oddly, we both wanted the same basic things. I speak of this gentleman because of something he said that impacted my entire view of mission and living. In his home country of Jamaica, he said, it's common to see an eighty-year-old man riding his bike to work every morning. Older Jamaicans don't work long days, but they still go to work each day and work, not because they must but because that's what they do—it's their mission.

In the West, America especially, we tend to overwhelmingly direct our mission in light of worldly success. This includes getting or developing wealth, increasing in power, affluence, and influence, and the list goes on. The problem with success is that it's a terrible north star for determining or defining our mission.

YOUR GOD MISSION

It's easy to be blessed and then forget about what someone else or even what God did for us, whether we have been Christians a long time or a short time. As new believers in Christ, we tend to immerse ourselves deeply in a Christ-community, which is wise and necessary. But sometimes we withdraw from the world and never go back to visit. Once saved, we are to be in Christian community, but we must also get out of the community to share our faith with the unsaved world.

While many Christians become deeply immersed in Christian culture and retreat from the world, Jesus made clear that after God saves us there is work to be done. Mark 5 tells the story of Jesus casting out the legion of demons from a man so demon-possessed that he broke out of and destroyed the iron shackles the authorities continually put on his body to restrain him. While this may seem like a lot of power, the power of God through Christ is stronger. The Jewish pig owners were scared because they feared losing more revenue from more dead pigs. The man with many demons, called "Legion," responded to Jesus with a grateful heart.

Notice the different responses from people who saw and experienced the same event. While the man with the demons experienced the miracle directly, others saw it in real time. Mark 5 says:

> *As he [Jesus] was getting into the boat the man who had been possessed with demons begged him that he might be with him. And he [Jesus] did not permit him but said to him, "Go home to your friends and tell them how much the Lord has done for you, and how he has had mercy on you." And he went away and began to proclaim in the Decapolis how much Jesus had done for him, and everyone marveled.* (Mark 5:18–20)

It's easy to read this short passage without seeing all God is telling us as to why Jesus wouldn't allow the man healed of a legion of demons to join Him as one of His disciples. Let's break this down into three simple points.

First, the request: The man freed from a legion of demons begged Jesus to let him join Him and His disciples (v.18), but Jesus denied him. We often ask God for things in prayer that the Lord seems to deny or not answer. God does not do this out of a mean heart but out of love and His much greater plan for us. His plans are not ours. In Isaiah 55:8–9 God says, *"My plans aren't your plans, nor are your ways my ways, says the Lord. Just as the heavens are higher than the earth, so are my ways higher than your ways, and my plans than your plans"* (CEB). Simply put, God has something ever better and greater than we ask for in many cases. As finite creatures, we often cannot see the big picture, and God has so much more for us than we can see in the moment of our requests. We may pray for a spouse, a job, ministry, or other things, but God often gives us something very different than what we ask for. And He does so in part, but not in whole, to fulfill His purpose and mission for our life.

Second, the mission: Jesus denied the request of newly freed man for two specific reasons. In the words of Scripture: *And he [Jesus] did not permit him but said to him, "Go home to your friends and* ***tell them*** *how much the Lord has done for you, and how much he [God] had mercy on you"* (v. 19, emphasis added).

Jesus didn't just deny this newly saved man or abruptly leave him. Instead, Jesus called him to mission and life purpose in that he was to go home on mission to his friends and do a few specific things. First, this man was to "tell them" (his home region of ten cities!) how much the Lord had done for him, and he was to show the people of those cities that God is a merciful God as was demonstrated in Jesus healing and freeing him from the many demons. When God calls us to mission and purpose, it always comes with some level of focus and specific tasks. Not that it can't also be broad in scope, but God calls us to specific mission and purpose. What is the mission(s) God called you to?

Third, the response: *And he [the man] went away and began to proclaim in the Decapolis how much Jesus had done for him, and everyone marveled* (v. 20). What's so important about Jesus sending the man home? Jesus obviously knew where his home was, and that home was an important place. Decapolis is the region southeast of the Sea of Galilee, where (at that time) were ten cities (the number varied over history). During that time, the ten cities of Decapolis and the surrounding region were inhabited mostly by Gentiles, not Jews. Did Jesus send the man home to retire and chill out, enjoy life, and go to church, never to return to the PTSD of being possessed by many demons? No. God called him to mission. And God calls you and me to mission as well.

I think it safe to say that Jesus had a mission-purpose for this man who was so thankful and grateful for being freed from a legion of demons that he was on figurative fire for the Lord. This man met the God of the universe and simply wanted to share that with the part of the world God called him to. That was this man's specific mission. And it was an important mission field. Decapolis had a strong Greek influence, meaning the people in those cities served many false gods through polytheism (worship of many gods) using idols. Jesus gave this guy a large mission field of ten cities full of unsaved people!

WHY GOD BROUGHT YOU INTO THIS WORLD

Our life mission is one of the most important elements of living. It's in great part why God brought us into this world. We are on earth to fulfill a mission centered on participating in God's mission of redemption and restoration through spreading the message of His love and the teachings of Jesus Christ. Christians are called to be messengers and ambassadors for God, sharing the good news of Jesus's life, death, and resurrection. This mission aims to bring people into a right relationship with God and to restore all of creation.

Jesus made clear in Matthew 16 that He came with a mission to the point of confronting Peter's non-suspecting resistance to that mission in taking Jesus aside and wrongly rebuking Jesus out of what Peter thought was love. Jesus has just said that *he must go to Jerusalem and suffer many things from the elders and chief priests and scribes, and be killed* (v. 21). Verse 22 says, *And Peter took Him [Jesus] aside and began to rebuke him, saying "Far be it from you, Lord! This shall never happen to you."* By "this," Peter meant that such a horrible thing—death—should never happen to Jesus. But in verse 23, Jesus gives Peter a sharp, direct reply:

> *But He turned and said to Peter, "Get behind me, Satan! You are a hindrance to me. For you are not setting your mind on the things of God, but on the things of man." Then Jesus told his disciples, "If anyone would come after me, let him deny himself and take up his cross and follow me. For whoever would save his life will lose it, but whoever loses his life for my sake will find it. For what will it profit a man if he gains the whole world but forfeits his soul."* (Matthew 16:23–25)

Jesus made clear to Peter that He came to earth with a very specific mission, which included becoming the sacrifice and payment for our sins. Jesus sharply rebuked Peter for unknowingly aligning himself with Satan's plan to deter Jesus from fulfilling His mission. The harshness of Jesus's rebuke stems from His fierce realism about the principal purpose of His coming to earth—to die—which to many is a hindrance, *a stone of stumbling, and a rock of offense* (Romans 9:33).

To call Peter Satan was a serious accusation. But when Peter stood in the way of God's plan (the mission of Christ), he was speaking for Satan. The mouth that was used as the vehicle of God's oracle became the channel of Satan's lie. How fickle we can be as people. And how patient God is with us. This incident with Peter illustrates the importance and urgency of our focus on living out our life with purpose, meaning, and most importantly, through mission. If we fail to live out our purpose and meaning, what is the value of that purpose and meaning?

Let's be careful to remember where we came from and that God has a mission for our life. Let's not be distracted by the comforts, conveniences, and recreation our modern age offers us. Be careful not to withdraw from seeking God's purpose, meaning, and mission for your life. Instead, accept the exciting mission He has called you to from eternity, which will determine your destination.

10

THE ANCIENT IDEA OF MISSION

Expect great things from God.
Attempt great things for God. [65]
–William Carey

My Italian parents and grandparents often spoke in parables. After I trusted Jesus Christ as my Lord and Savior, I discovered that many of the principled parables my mother taught me growing up were biblical. She said things like, "Steven, a tiger can't change its stripes." Generally speaking, she was right. People don't change. They have the ability to change, especially if they are transformed by Christ and the Christian faith. But many choose not to change. My mother's wisdom served me very well. While she never explicitly connected that wisdom to the Bible, Jeremiah 13:23 says, *Can the Ethiopian change his skin or the leopard his spots? Then also you can do good who are accustomed to do evil.* In this chapter, we'll look into biblical wisdom literature in an effort to help us understand mission from the ancients who lived thousands of years ago. Why? Ancient wisdom doesn't change, because wisdom comes from God and He doesn't change (Malachi 3:6).

Anyone, including those who do not believe in God, can pick up this book and benefit from it. But the very best direction for your life mission, one filled with meaning and purpose, can only be found in

God's eternal plan for your life. First, God's plan is far better than ours. For example, the land of Canaan was never meant to be the ultimate resting place of God's people. God always had a better plan in mind. Second, God's plan is far more expansive than we can grasp. As believers, we have been commissioned by Christ to go to the ends of the earth sharing the gospel, baptizing, and making disciples (Matthew 11:28–30). Third, God's plan is older than we can imagine, better than we can dream, more expansive than we can grasp, and beyond our ability to fully comprehend. That is why this book is centered on His Book (the Bible) as the primary authority for life purpose, meaning, and mission.

I have provided a consistent theme throughout this book regarding Who makes our plans from eternity and where true wisdom to discover our purpose, meaning, and mission comes from. The Who is God and the source text for wisdom and discovery is the Holy Bible. You will not find such wisdom in any other book. This is why I have cited the ancient King Solomon frequently:

> *And God gave Solomon wisdom and understanding beyond measure, and breadth of mind like the sand on the seashore, so that Solomon's wisdom surpassed the wisdom of all the people of the east and all the wisdom of Egypt. For he was wiser than all other men, wiser than Ethan the Ezrahite, and Heman, Calcol, and Darda, the sons of Mahol, and his fame was in all the surrounding nations. He also spoke 3,000 proverbs, and his songs were 1,005. He spoke of trees, from the cedar that is in Lebanon to the hyssop that grows out of the wall. He spoke also of beasts, and of birds, and of reptiles, and of fish. And people of all nations came to hear the wisdom of Solomon, and from all the kings of the earth, who had heard of his wisdom.* (1 Kings 4:29–34)

As a man *wiser than all other men* of his era, Solomon gave us his wise conclusion that there is nothing better in life than for us to seek God's mission for our life with purpose and meaning: *So I saw that there is nothing better than that a man should rejoice in his work, for that is his lot. Who can bring him to see what will be after him?* (Ecclesiastes 3:22). Again, I share this with you for one reason: the ancient wisdom literature of the Bible is the best source for us to ultimately gain what we need in the most truthful, accurate, well-conceived way. That said, the New Testament Scriptures hold much wisdom as well. Let's take a look at the book of Mark for the simple reason that Mark is a book of action and purpose, meaning and mission.

NEW TESTAMENT WISDOM

In the New Testament, the book of Mark is unique in that this gospel emphasizes what Jesus did, meaning His mission, rather than what He said. It is a book of action. The Greek word *euthsus*, usually translated or "at once" or "immediately," occurs more than forty times in the book, emphasizing Mark's important mission of communicating the mission of Jesus in motion. While Jesus is the ultimate Servant Leader, His disciples were also servant leaders; you and I are too if we are followers of Jesus Christ. The theme of Mark is Christ the Servant. The key verse is 10:45 where Jesus says, "*For even the Son of Man came not to be served but to serve, and to give his life as a ransom for many.*" Mark speaks to the service (mission) of Jesus as the Servant (1:1–10:52) and the sacrifice of Jesus as the Servant (11:1–16:20).

Jesus lived only thirty-three years in his human, earthly body. This shows us, first, that life is short and while on this earth, despite our age, our mission never expires. Second, Jesus modeled for us that living out our mission means being a servant leader (not a boss). Hence, our overall mission is to serve God and others no matter what specific mission we have been called to. And remember, we can use all that God has given us to either glorify Him or to exalt ourselves.

Living out our specific life mission can take many forms—running a business, being a parent, serving in the government, or any other mission we can imagine. If we serve God in mission driven by purpose and meaning, we will hit the mark in life and be fulfilled in good times and in bad times all the way into eternity. What we want to avoid is thinking that we have lived a successful, mission-driven life when in fact we have missed the mark by living for selfish gain focused only on temporal things without taking action that will last into eternity.

AVOID WASTED HUMAN POTENTIAL

Imagine what our world and eternal destiny would be like if Jesus had not put into motion or completed His mission. Because we are beings created in His image, the same in application can be said of you and me. One of the saddest things for me to observe is the wasted capital and forfeiture of human potential and a fulfilled life. Some of the categories that fill this space are people in both the private sector and government who do not work hard because they are not pushed, challenged, or have benchmarks that stretch them beyond simply doing a job or task. Other categories include those on perpetual welfare: especially those who have been led to depend on government money as opposed to being pushed to achieve all God has for them. How many doctors, leaders, businesspeople, and godly parents have not developed fully, if at all, due to their dependency on others? They have not been stretched to achieve all God has for them to be and do so they can help the truly needy people of this world (not those who game it).

All people—of all cultures, races, color, and backgrounds—have value, purpose, meaning, and mission. So why do so many millions of people choose to take the easy road? As sinful human beings, we often tend to do only what we must in life to get by. In America, it's easy to work too little or too much because the financial reward is so attractive for both the rich and poor. But a balance is achievable for those who seek wisdom in the right place.

That said, I want to return to the Old Testament Jewish Scriptures and again look to King Solomon. While he wrote several books in the Bible, one of the most interesting ones is Ecclesiastes, because he wrote it at the end of his life. My former mentor Dr. Barry Leventhal said to me once as we left our lunch meeting, "It's easy to see God in the rearview [mirror]." Solomon was looking in his rearview mirror when he wrote Ecclesiastes.

LOOKING IN LIFE'S REARVIEW MIRROR

In Ecclesiastes, as Solomon reflects on his wealth, accomplishments, and wisdom, he concludes that life is meaningless unless it is aligned with God's purpose, meaning, and mission. My challenge to you is to read Solomon's words carefully and then determine to live out God's purpose for your life with greater meaning through mission until He calls you home. If you do that, you will experience supernatural peace, fulfillment, and eternal purpose. To do only what is expected is not only a waste of capital but also a sad state of forfeiting all you could have been and possibly still can be in this life and for eternity.

LIVE OUT YOUR MISSION WITH ALL YOUR MIGHT

Solomon wrote in Ecclesiastes 9:10, *Whatever your hand finds to do, do it with all your might, for there is no work or thought or knowledge or wisdom in Sheol [death], to which you are going.* Though much of life is futile, Solomon says that one must grasp its opportunities to the fullest in serving God. This should lead us to re-evaluate our life purpose and meaning for the simple reason that thinking through such a mission leads to actionable mission—how we live out what we understand as our purpose and meaning.

One of my best of friends from college in Washington, DC, was promoted to a high position and told me that he doesn't want to end up like his boss who retired at age seventy-two. My friend bumped into the retired executive, who was in his mid-seventies, at a condominium in Crystal City, Virginia, and asked him how he liked retirement. The man said he does water aerobics daily as his main focus. Some might be tempted to think such a life is the reward of hard work. I would assert that a life void of purpose, meaning, and mission is like a horse put out to pasture until it dies. There is nothing exciting, rewarding, or fulfilling in that. A stagnant life void of some level of mission is not a meaningful living.

Solomon reminds us that we have a short, limited window in life, and once that window closes, there will be no opportunities to pursue mission. If we view success from purely a secular or humanistic perspective, we limit our ability to work toward a fulfilled life here and in eternity. When we work strictly for ourselves, we work only for the temporal with no long-term investment for our eternal existence. As Jesus said in Matthew 6:19–21,

> *Do not lay up for yourselves treasures on earth, where moth and rust destroy and where thieves break in and steal, but lay up for yourselves treasures in heaven, where neither moth nor rust destroys and where thieves do not break in and steal. For where your treasure is, there your heart will be also.*

Hence, how we view success determines how we live out our life mission, and how we live out our mission is essential to our existence in eternity. I pray you will consider the Bible's ancient wisdom literature—both the New Testament and Old Testament—in your search for purpose, meaning, and mission. So far, everything I've said in this book hinges on one simple question: "Whom do you serve?" Your answer to this question dictates how you live out your life purpose and mission. So ask yourself, "Whom am I serving?"

11

WHOM DO YOU SERVE?

It is high time we change the ideal of success for the ideal of serve.[66]
–Albert Einstein

In November 2024, I flew to McLean, Virginia, for a donor meeting with the help of my friend Patricia and other great friends and supporters of my ministry ReasonForTruth.org to update and expand our supporters. Afterward, I called Patricia to thank her for helping me with all the logistics, which included supplying all the food and beverages. During our conversation, Patricia said, "Steve, the key issue is who we serve." I paused to ingest that statement, to process it because she was spot on. Discovering meaning in one's life leads to purpose. Once we discover that purpose, we are finally able to move that purpose through action (a verb). This is called our mission. And we cannot discover meaning, purpose, or mission without asking the all-encompassing question of whom we truly serve. That realization defines what we consider to be true life meaning. Our mission automatically flows from there.

Where do you find your meaning? Is it in your children, job, ministry? Many of us find our meaning in our wealth, talents, influence, affluence, and the opportunity to use these temporal blessings. There is no neutral way to use these blessings because they are either used for good or bad. When used for God, whether directly or indirectly, they are good. And this is the elephant in the room. Patricia brought up the example of feeding the poor. While that is a noble activity, it has no eternal meaning or purpose if it only serves the physical self. In Patricia's case, she uses her wealth for good through a coffee shop ministry, Reason For Truth, and her church, which all point people to Jesus.

ONLY TWO OPTIONS

What do I mean by whom we serve? We can break the answer into many subcategories, but the only two options are serving God or serving ourselves. For example, a friend I grew up with called me and said he wanted to pick my brain about a Christian food truck ministry for the poor. I asked, "What *exactly* do you want to feed them?" He said sandwiches, drinks, and the like. I said, "That's not enough." If he fills the stomach, the stomach will become hungry again in a matter of hours. If he fills them spiritually, they will be eternally satisfied.

Consider the story of the Samaritan woman recorded in the Gospel of John:

> *The woman said to him, "Sir, you have nothing to draw water with, and the well is deep. Where do you get that living water? Are you greater than our father Jacob? He gave us the well and drank from it himself, as did his sons and his livestock." Jesus said to her, "Everyone who drinks of this water will be thirsty again, but whoever drinks of the water that I will give him will never be thirsty again. The water that I will give him will become in him a spring of water welling up to eternal life." The woman said to him, "Sir, give me this water, so that I will not be thirsty or have to come here to draw water."* (John 4:11–15)

Jesus was far more interested in the woman's eternal thirst—her need for God—than her temporal thirst. My friend gave me the temporal, incorrect answer. Again, I asked him, "What do you want to feed them biblically and spiritually, and how do you plan to execute that through mission?" He pushed back on me because he had no answer. I explained that feeding the poor is a noble idea. I'm sure it would have given him some meaning, purpose, and even mission but on a limited level. When our mission carries no eternal meaning or purpose (void of the message of the Christian faith) we are serving our own desires, not those of God. To help you move from purpose to meaning to mission, I will provide a basic blueprint of ideas in this chapter that can help you get there.

A CORE PRINCIPLE OF MISSION

Being a Christian involves serving others, as it is a core principle and command within Christianity, exemplified by Jesus Christ's life of service and teachings. Christians are called to serve out of love and humility, acting as a reflection of Christ's heart and the core tenets of Christian faith, with the belief that such service brings glory to God. When we do this selflessly, it has a transformative impact on both the servant and the recipient. Here are five good reasons that we serve others to keep in mind:

1) Follow Jesus's example of servant leadership. He said, "*The Son of Man came not to be served but to serve, and to give his life as a ransom for many.*" (Mark 10:45)
2) Keep God's commands. Paul wrote, *For you were called to freedom, brothers. Only do not use your freedom as an opportunity for the flesh, but through love serve one another.* (Galatians 5:13)
3) Live out love for God and others. Serving others is a simple, tangible way to express the unconditional *agape* love (the steadfast, unconditional love) God gives us. Jesus said, "*As I have loved you, you also are to love one another. By this all people will know that you are my disciples, if you have love for one another*" (John 13:34–35).
4) Serving God with the right heart bears witness to Christ. When we serve God rightly, with the right motives, our good works shine a light on our faith. As a result, God will use us to lead

others to Him through Christ. Jesus said, *"Let your light shine before others, so that they may see you good works and give glory to our Father who is in heaven"* (Matthew 5:16).

5) Serving nurtures spiritual growth. By serving others, we fuel our own spiritual growth and development. When we serve others in the name of Christ, we give glory to God: *Whoever serves, as one who serves by the strength that God supplies—in order that in everything God may be glorified through Jesus Christ* (1 Peter 4:11).

When we serve others with acts of practical everyday help, with a humble attitude, and a sacrificial spirit, using the resources God has given us for His glory, our serving moves from the temporal to the eternal. In the end, serving God above all other things in this world and our own desires aligns with the biblical principle of prioritizing God's kingdom and righteousness. This is what Jesus taught as He commanded His followers to love and serve God supremely, even above one's closest family. *Then Jesus said to him, "Be gone, Satan! For it is written, "You shall worship the Lord your God and him only shall you* ***serve****"* (Matthew 4:10 emphasis added).

In the first of the Ten Commandments given through Moses, God made clear, *"You shall have no other gods before me"* (Exodus 20:3). This commandment leads us to a commitment that involves placing God at the forefront of all decisions and relationships. With God as our starting point, our purpose will reflect that as our meaning is defined through God. As a result, it all works out through the mission God has for us in each stage of life. And sadly, in some cases, friends of old sometimes fade so God can shine more brightly in our life. As a consequence, through that fading we depend more deeply on God and see His purpose and mission more clearly.

12

FRIENDS FADE SO GOD CAN SHINE

Not only does God give us a new relationship with Himself
and make us citizens of His kingdom,
but He also gives us a new family—the family of God [67]
–Billy Graham

When I passed the age of sixty, I started thinking more deeply about making the most out of the remaining time I have left on this earth. My prayer is that God gives me many more decades to serve Him in my life purpose and help my wife and children go as far as they can with what God gives. I didn't panic when I entered my sixties, but I felt a new sense of urgency to live out my life purpose and mission.

The average age of the CEOs of top Fortune 500 companies is sixty-two, and the average age of pastors of the 100 largest U.S. churches is seventy-one.[68] As the years pass, especially at or around age sixty, our life purpose changes. And so does our purpose-mission. God deliberately prunes some of our old relationships, allowing and drawing us to home in on and grow more deeply in our relationships with Him and a limited number of our remaining friends. Our time with the Lord, through our study of His Word and through prayer, becomes richer and more meaningful in relationship with Him instead of wide-open and energy-driven without connecting with Him. This can be painful as we watch long-time friends, and sadly sometimes family members, grow more distant from us. This distance is often fueled by their moving further from God while we perhaps grow closer to Him.

I wrote about this topic in a recent podcast and will speak to it later in the chapter. John MacArthur masterfully addressed this subject in a podcast as well. That podcast helped form this chapter as it clarifies why some relationships grow cold in our latter years. MacArthur explains the reasons for such distancing as (1) God drawing us closer to Him for a richer, deeper, more meaningful relationship in Him and (2) God desiring to refocus or recalibrate our mission in the latter part of our life.

In our younger years, we serve with energy, youthfulness, and the burning desire to work full-on at building our ministry, reputation, and wealth as our main purpose. In other words, our meaning, purpose, and mission during that time are driven more by carnal/earthly desires for purpose, meaning, and mission. In contrast, in our latter years, God refocuses us on what matters most. He moves us closer to Himself and a smaller subset of people while moving us away from many people we might consider acquaintances (sometimes misunderstood and mislabeled as friends).

I'm not saying we are to become recluses and withdraw from people, community, fellowship, or family. What I am saying, though, is that God will have us focus on fewer things and people. At this turning point, we downsize our homes because our children are gone. We no longer seek to build on our wealth, a professional network, or a reputation at the cost of being away from home so much. We spend less time and energy on trying to change the world and our personal holdings (whether ministerial or materially). God slows us down on purpose to meet with Him and others in our circle on a much deeper level. In this stage, we should be focusing on building our relationship with God and pouring into the next generation to pick up where we are leaving off. We may not be on earth tomorrow, so it's better to live each day as if it's our last.

God puts that thought on our heart and mind, but it's ours to accept or reject. In the end, our purpose and our perception of a meaningful life change. As a result, our life mission changes too.

A LESSON IN FOCUS AND ACCURACY

This shift is God's way of pruning our desire for social events, ministry missions, and service to Him. Anyone around or over sixty can attest to the fact that energy fades as the years go by. We are living longer and stronger, but we can't do at age sixty or older what we did at age thirty. When I was in my early twenties, I played competitive racquetball at the University of Maryland (UMCP). I played with the UMCP racquetball team weekly but was not on the team. One day I was playing with a group of older men, who taught me a powerful lesson. I came onto the court ready to compete and tear up the two older guys. They looked like something out of the 1970s with their old-style head bands, wrist bands, old-style shorts, and tall socks with a red stripe. I laughed to myself, thinking I was going to have some fun with them.

I was allowed to serve, and the games began. I ran around like a cat on catnip. I was all over the court, full-on with endless energy. I played well but with less precision than the older guys. Then everything changed. One of the older opponents, moving very little within a confined space, started placing the racquetball with an impressive degree of accuracy—consistently placing it an inch off the floor. I was left frozen in time as the ball simply dribbled by me in slow motion. I stopped running around the court like a wild beast as he placed the kill shot with ease. This is how God designed us to be. As we get older, life is not so much about high energy as it is about experience, wisdom, and character. It's not about how many speaking engagements we book or how many downloads our podcast or YouTube channel gets. That is worldly thinking. Life becomes more about doing the fewer, simpler but more important things God has for us to do. It's about serving God, serving others, and using the time and energy God has loaned us to be in relationship with Him more deeply and to execute our God-given mission more accurately according to His will as opposed to our will.

REDEFINING MISSION

In our latter years, life is not about energy or ego but about God's purpose for our life, which gives us true, eternal meaning. And this process of redefining how we see and live out life in light of God's purpose materializes in honing our mission to be less broad, less ego-driven, and more focused with a listening ear to God's well-placed mission, which in turn glorifies Him. It's a time to serve God for His glory as opposed to our self-image or perception thereof. It should not be about attention and accolades like a mid-life crisis but about humbling ourselves before our Lord in service to Him and others. Those things we chased in our youth are not to be the same goals in our latter years. As we mature, God begins a new work in us. As a result, we begin to better understand the words of older Paul to younger Timothy in a whole new light: *I have fought the good fight, I have finished the race, I have kept the faith* (2 Timothy 4:7).

We also begin to see God working in our life in a new way. That said, this process can take place in our earlier years to a lesser degree if we allow God to use us more simply. When we are young, though, God gives us youth, energy, drive, and desire to go full throttle for His purpose lived out through mission. And that mission is most important, as God tells us through the parable of the talents in Matthew 25.

In this parable, God makes clear that there are three types of people in this world: those who stayed the course of faith, those who never entered the course to begin with, and then there are those who started strong but finished poorly or didn't finish at all. In this parable, two of the servants received the same reward, indicating faithfulness in the use of the different abilities given to them. Both did well and multiplied what God gave them faithfully. The third servant, though, is condemned for his sloth and indifference. Had the third, slothful servant only kept his eye on the kingdom of God and had the heart and determination to do well with what God had given him at that point in his life, he would have been blessed by God, our Master, and given more. Instead, God admonishes and demotes him.

> *Now after a long time the master of those servants came and settled accounts with them. And he who had received the five talents came forward, bringing five talents more, saying, "Master, you delivered to me five talents; here, I have made five talents more." His master said to him, "Well done, good and faithful servant. You have been faithful over a little; I will set you over much. Enter into the joy of your master." And he also who had the two talents came forward, saying, "Master, you delivered to me two talents; here, I have made two talents more." His master said to him, "Well done, good and faithful servant. You have been faithful over a little; I will set you over much. Enter into the joy of your master." He also who had received the one talent came forward, saying, "Master, I knew you to be a hard man, reaping where you did not sow, and gathering where you scattered no seed, so I was afraid, and I went and hid your talent in the ground. Here, you have what is yours." But his master answered him, "You wicked and slothful servant! You knew that I reap where I have not sown and gather where I scattered no seed? Then you ought to have invested my money with the bankers, and at my coming I should have received what was my own with interest. So take the talent from him and give it to him who has the ten talents. For to everyone who has will more be given, and he will have an abundance. But from the one who has not, even what he has will be taken away. And cast the worthless servant into the outer darkness. In that place there will be weeping and gnashing of teeth."* (Matthew 25:19–30)

A mission-focused life is all about what we do with what God has given us at each stage. And God expects something different from us during each stage. As we advance in years, some of our friends will pass away, but God will separate us from others. In other words, life is constantly changing, and we must be open to God's leading at each stage. This is all part of God's purpose for our lives. This entails God's pruning the relationships that most likely are not the best for us.

Here's a summary of John MacArthur's message on this topic:

> *Why does God sometimes isolate us as we grow older, especially after 60? In this thought-provoking message, Pastor John MacArthur explores the divine reasons behind spiritual separation, isolation, and pruning in later life. If you're wondering why certain relationships have faded or why you feel more alone in this season, this sermon offers deep biblical wisdom, comfort, and purpose.*
>
> *God uses solitude to shape your character, redirect your calling, and deepen your connection with Him. This is not only true for those over 60—it's for anyone who seeks to understand the purpose behind divine disconnection and spiritual refinement. Whether you're navigating loneliness, retirement, or a change in your circle, this video reveals what God may be doing behind the scenes—and why it's for your ultimate good*" (emphasis added).[69]

WHY SOME FAMILIES AND FRIENDS GROW DISTANT

In a ReasonForTruth.org podcast I recorded in August 2025, I addressed the subject biblically from a slightly different perspective yet still considering what MacArthur said. This is what I recorded:

Have you been wondering why some friends and family have grown distant or out of touch all together over the years, especially since the COVID-19 pandemic? Friendships of old sometimes fade for Christians as well as non-Christians. This is a spiritual issue more than a friendship issue.

A couple of my friends from old have gone radio silent over the past few years. This has baffled me because I cherish history and friendship like family. On the flip side, I speak weekly with a couple of other friends that I didn't spend nearly as much time with back in the '80s. Why? I realized that the two friends who call me weekly are growing daily in their biblical faith while the other two are moving away from Christ in their daily life. It's as simple as that. It's not an issue of friendship as much as it is about faith. I love my two distant friends and miss them dearly, but God always provides, and I'm cherishing my newer friends of old. Thank You, God, for Your provision of friendships. I am greatly blessed in riches of authentic faith in Christ and friends of faith.

Remember what Jesus said about who his family members are in the Gospel of Matthew:

> *While Jesus was still talking to the crowd, his mother and brothers stood outside, wanting to speak to him. Someone told him, "Your mother and brothers are standing outside, wanting to speak to you." He replied to him, "Who is my mother, and who are my brothers?" Pointing to his disciples, he said, "Here are my mother and my brothers. For whoever does the will of my Father in heaven is my brother and sister and mother."* (Matthew 12:46–50 NIV)

Jesus is not saying that our blood family is the same as our spiritual family. They are not. When our earthly, bloodline family is following God through Christ, that's the best of both worlds! In the Old Testament Scriptures, ancient society was clear about this and placed great emphasis on faithfulness to blood relatives. Consider what the daughters of Zelophehad said to Moses:

> *"Why should the name of our father be taken away from his clan because he had no son? Give to us a possession among our father's brothers."* (Number 27:4)

In the Italian culture, we say blood is thicker than water, and we mean it. For Christians this is also true, except for the fact that we ultimately stand under the Federal Headship of Jesus Christ. In other words, God is more important than our earthly family. Unfortunately, some abuse this view in a wrong, ungodly way.

Jesus's words in Matthew 12:48–50 must have sounded quite foreign to the crowd, as the family unit was viewed as more important all other things, including God, for most people in that culture. But in that passage, Jesus didn't deny that the woman and the men at the door were His family. He merely pushed beyond the normal understanding of family to a larger reality—the claims of spiritual kinship. The new family included anyone who did the will of His Father in heaven. Far from denying the value or benefits of solid family relationships, Jesus (by calling attention to His Father) was underscoring the significance of family.

This passage was written to encourage people to follow Jesus, even in an environment of animosity. Jesus is making the point that being a follower of Jesus supersedes family commitment, and those who follow are adopted into a new family with God as their Father (Romans 8:15–17). This doesn't mean we put our family aside while we spend all our time at church to the detriment of family, though. That is selfish ambition and fulfilling our fleshly desires. What this means is that the spiritual relation between Christ and believers is closer than the closest of blood ties and the best of friends. Obedience to God takes precedence over our responsibilities to family. When our family is committed to the person of Jesus Christ, again, that's the best of both worlds. I have some of that myself by God's grace.

The simple truth is that some friendships, and sadly some family members, grow distant or separate from us altogether because we are growing closer to or further from Christ. It's as simple as that. We should pray for our family and friends that do not know Jesus Christ as Lord and Savior or who may have walked away or grown distant from our Lord. We need to love our family and friends while growing in our relationships with those who are growing closer to us in and through Jesus Christ.

I encourage you to embrace the simple truth that this is a spiritual issue more than a friendship or family issue. Doing so will provide you with greater clarity and peace as to why friendships and family ties sometimes grow faint or disappear over the years. And when this happens, realize that God is allowing it to recalibrate the next chapter He has for your purpose-filled mission.

13

DON'T RETIRE, RECALIBRATE

Retirement is not the end of the road.
It is the beginning of the open highway.[70]
–Unknown

As I write this book, many friends are retiring or talking about doing so in the near future. Such conversations seem strange, but they're a reality of growing older. My friend, mentor, and teacher, the late Dr. Norman Geisler, started Southern Evangelical Seminar (SES) in 1992. I remember him fondly because he began teaching and discipling me in 1999. He was a powerhouse—sharp as a tack, full of energy. On one occasion, soon after he turned eighty, we went to lunch, and I could barely keep up with him. Shortly thereafter, he began to slow down, but his wisdom kept steady.

We talked about wisdom in the previous chapter. In this one, I want to speak to putting all that God has given us into a purpose-filled mission in an effort to end our earthly life with a massive positive impact on others for His glory and their betterment. If we retire mainly to play golf or tennis as our end game, we let the best we have been given and worked for go unused and eventually disappear. We either use it or lose it before we are too old to remember it. This leads us to examine our purpose in retirement.

Illustrations are often helpful in helping us see truth, so allow me to use retired railroad trains as a way to learn about purpose, meaning, and mission after our workforce years end. When trains are retired for newer, more efficient models, they are seldom destined for the scrapyard. Instead, like human retirees, they are often repurposed. They may be reused by smaller railroad lines, converted to maintenance vehicles, sold for parts, or even recycled for raw metal. A small percentage of trains with an iconic model status may get historical status to mark the end of an era, but that's rare. As for humans, retirement is like a train changing its route to a slower, more scenic view instead of an urban speed route restricted by a time schedule and focused on high levels of profit and productivity. Like trains, people should change course and repurpose their lives instead of retiring to the train graveyard.

After years of pondering what retirement years should look like, I've concluded that retirement is not biblical, but semi-retirement is. Semi-retirement is simply taking a slower and more meaningful journey as you live out your life mission. Retirement is about adjustment and recalibration, a change that has pros and cons. The cons can be mitigated by retirees living out their new mission with meaning and purpose. In any case, many dramatic changes come with retirement—spiritual, physical, and psychological ones. Let's look at five major adjustments most all retirees face.

RETIREMENT ADJUSTMENTS

First, retirement often entails the loss of purpose and identity. For many people, life is defined by their career, which in turn defines their sense of purpose, structure, and identity. I once asked a gentleman at the gym what his retirement was like. He said, "Every day is Saturday except for Sunday." In other words, for him every day in retirement is the same as he lives a life of daily micro-movements but one that is void of any real big-picture mission for the week. I concluded that the difficulty of starting a new week on Monday is what makes Friday the best day of the week. In other words, Friday means mission accomplished for the week. As a reward, Friday is the signal to relax, rest, enjoy some recreation, and spend time with the family.

Second, retirement can lead to social isolation and loneliness. Leaving the workplace often means you no longer interact regularly with work-related friends and contacts, especially if they are still working.

Third, retirement can potentially lead to negative health impacts. A good friend from elementary school told me a number of years ago that his father's idea of retirement was sitting in his lounge chair watching television. He said that as the years passed, his father's hands crumpled with atrophy from lack of use. They were marked by the wasting away and shrinking of body tissue cells due to lack of nerve supply. In other words, the weakening of his hand muscles and tendons led to the functional loss of ability to move his hands, due to insufficient movement and exercise. Loss of mental functionality followed. Many studies have linked retirement to a sedentary lifestyle, which leads to reduced cognitive engagement, often resulting in depression, anxiety, and heart problems. The logical conclusion is that cognitive decline is likely to follow when retirees fail to stay active physically, mentally, and spiritually.

Fourth, retirement can lead to difficulty adjusting to unstructured time. When every day becomes Saturday, we lose important markers that give us purpose, meaning, and mission. How can we have any sense of purpose or mission if we have no consistent markers in our day or week? We can't. For many, leaving the workforce is a transition from a highly structured schedule (day, week, and month) to a frameless blob of unstructured time. Challenging for most people, this can lead to feeling less productive, more unmotivated, and less valued.

Fifth, retirement often takes on a stigma or misperception of laziness due to the retiree's lifestyle. Making friends and developing new social groups may also be more difficult, which creates a whole new cycle of negative consequences for a retirement that lacks purpose, meaning, and mission.[71] But retirement offers many benefits too.

PROS OF RETIREMENT

Retirement gives the freedom of flexibility. This includes time for hobbies, travel, family gatherings, and opportunities to serve God and others. Retirement can be a time of reduced stress in your life—which is good to a degree (see chapter 3). This season of life can lead to learning new things and focusing on your personal health. It may provide time to create a life filled with joy, peace, and new meaning. An article in *Farther Financial,* titled "The Pros and Cons of Early Retirement," highlighted several benefits. Let's look at four of them.

First, retirement is a time of freedom and increased personal time, which can allow you to escape the confinement of work schedules and a demanding boss. Retirement allows the time to do the things we were unable to do pre-retirement. Almost every retiree I know says they are busier in retirement than they were in the workforce. But with that freedom comes the responsibility of self-structuring their day, schedule, and life. That can be stressful, but if done in the right way, it can lead to a more joyful life. This entails continued commitment to one's purpose, meaning, and mission.

Second, retirement is a time for lifestyle change and personal growth. It provides freedom from what we were obligated to do when we were in the workforce. It also allows us to do the things we always wanted to do but didn't have the time or resources to do.

Third, retirement is a time to regain better physical and mental health. Leaving a high-pace, pressure-filled job will lower your stress levels and anxiety. And taking on those hobbies, sports, and recreation may involve more physical activity. Hiking, eating healthier, and Pilates can lead to a better physical state to implement your mission. Retired life can and should be used to spend more time with family and friends. Family time and social interaction are essential to our mental, emotional, and spiritual well-being. This also helps mitigate the effects of loneliness that may come with retirement.

Fourth, if planned well, retired life can bring increased financial security. Many retired people downsize their homes, so they have much less to clean, maintain, and pay taxes on. This leads to a simpler and often better quality of life. Downsizing your home may mean getting rid of the big yard, the pool, and many other maintenance responsibilities.[72] A dear friend of my family, Mrs. Keating, said to me decades ago, "Steven, the more things you own, the more things own you." I'm not against owning nice things (and neither was she), but her meaning was clear: Simplification eliminates many of the monetary, mental, and meaningless things in life.

Retirement may also bring greater peace of mind due to the lack of workplace responsibilities. It means no longer having to dress for work, not to mention the financial cost of buying suitable, or necessary, work-life clothing.

AVOID BECOMING ROOTLESS

In "The Retreat of the Successful: Why Local Businesses Are Disappearing—and So Are the People Who Once Built Them," guest writer Justin Powell made the following comments on the Aaron Renn blog:

> *Even the retirees themselves don't gain as much as they think. Their calendars may be full, but they often feel rootless. Disconnected. You can't recreate the depth of a 30-year friendship at age 70 wandering around your empty vacation home. And when those familiar faces are no longer around, a kind of spiritual loneliness sets in. I'm not calling for people to die at their desks. But I am calling for them to finish well—to stay invested in the places that shaped them, to hand off what they've built with care, and to think generationally, not transactionally.*[73]

The great news is that thinking relationally with purpose, meaning, and mission in retirement leads to better health.

RETIREMENT WITH PURPOSE

In an earlier chapter, I mentioned a post on *The Epoch Times*, "Purposeful People Live Longer—and Better—According to Research," written by Dr. Yuhong Dong. In that article he also wrote about discovering or reducing dementia in the elderly. The study published in 2019 by *General Psychiatry* examined 951 seniors, with an average age of eighty, over seven years. During that time 155 persons, or 16.6 percent, contracted Alzheimer's disease. The study showed that people with a higher sense of purpose in life have a 51 percent lower risk of Alzheimer's disease compared to those with a lower purpose of life. The research team accounted for and made adjustments for a number of factors, including age, gender, and education level. The study also found that people who set higher (more difficult) life goals have a reduced risk of developing mild cognitive impairment (MCI) by 20 percent, which is a precursor to Alzheimer's disease. Lastly, the study found that establishing a life goal can benefit other aspects of health such as mortality in the elderly.

The article concluded that logotherapy—a psychotherapeutic approach that focuses on guiding people to find and discover the meaning of life, to establish clear goals in life, and to face and master life with a positive attitude—entails three important elements. The first element is the freedom of will, which has both spiritual and mental components. The second element is the will to seek life meaning, which was found to be the overall foundation of responsibility in one's life. (I submit that this is the antithesis of being taken care of by the state.) The will to seek life meaning is active and original to one's unique circumstances. The third and last element is embracing the meaning of life. This differs from person to person. If one doesn't like to think more deeply, they are very unlikely to discover the meaning of their life. In the end, the article points out that thought determines behavior, behavior determines character, and character determines destiny.[74] So why is retirement such a valued status in American life?

THE BIRTH OF MODERN-DAY RETIREMENT

The concept of modern retirement took off in the 1950s, although it began to take form between 1900–1920 with the advent of the industrial revolution. Older factory workers were viewed as less efficient than machines, so they were forced into retirement. This led to more unemployment and created pressure on state, local, and federal government officials to create pension plans and social programs. This ultimately led to the Social Security Act in 1935. Fast-forward twenty years, and the 1950s took retirement to a whole new level with the expansion of social security, which took the concept of retirement mainstream with greater popularity.[75]

Our modern idea of retirement was advanced as people in the United States became wealthier. With that wealth came access to a better quality of food, medical care, and transportation. Older generations lived longer and younger generations were financially capable of moving out and living on their own much sooner.

In the 1950s, retirement still only lasted around five to ten years before the person passed away. Over the past seventy years, due to medical advancements and other developments, the lifespan of most people has become longer. As a result, in some cases, people live in retirement for almost as long as they lived out their working life.

As of 2024, one of the fastest growing segments of American society is those over the age of eighty-five. Since many of them are (thankfully) in good health, they tend to focus on leisure (golf and travel), family (grandchildren), hobbies, and more relaxation. When kept in perspective regarding God's calling on their lives, longevity is good. But what does the Bible say about work and retirement?

THE BIBLICAL VIEW OF RETIREMENT

To gain a clear perspective on what the Bible says, we turn to the book of Genesis to see what God said about work to the first humans—Adam and Eve.

As I noted in chapter 4, when God created the first two humans, He gave them the garden of Eden as a workplace. Genesis 2:15 says, *The Lord God took the man and put him in the garden of Eden to work it and keep it.* This tells us that work was given to us in the beginning of time by God as part of creation—before Adam and Eve sinned. Thus, God created work as part of His original design for humanity. So, the Bible teaches that work has intrinsic value. Work was not by *the sweat of [Adam's] face* in the beginning. That came later (Genesis 3:19).

Second, after sin entered the world, work became more difficult and stressful. God called Adam to a life of strenuous work, saying, "*Cursed is the ground because of you; in pain shall you eat of it all the days of your life*" (Genesis 3:17). So, the Bible clearly teaches that the difficulty of work is a result of the Fall—Adam and Eve disobeying God and eating fruit from the Tree of the Knowledge of Good and Evil. Adam had worked in the garden before he and Eve ate the forbidden fruit. After they disobeyed God, they were judged by God and subjected to a new, more arduous life outside the garden.

Nowhere in the Bible does it say that any of us with the ability to work should ever stop working. This includes retirement. On the flip side, this does not mean that we ought to work until we die either. We are not to stop living with purpose, meaning, and mission—but the mission may change. The Christian should live with the goal of finishing life well. So, retirement or semi-retirement is a phase where we can use our God-given gifts, skills, and abilities to help others in our family, community, country, and throughout the world to glorify God differently than we did when we worked full-time. It is a time of recalibration. This doesn't mean we shouldn't enjoy life. We should enjoy all God has blessed us with. That may mean we play golf, travel, and relax in our later years. But it should also mean that we continue to glorify God and build His kingdom.

My teacher and mentor of nineteen years, Dr. Norman Geisler told me, "Steve, I will burn out, not rust out." At first, I thought he was a glutton for punishment, but as I grew older and wiser, I saw the wisdom in that a purposeful life never stops its mission. After Dr. Geisler passed away, a friend told me that he had spoken at her church a few weeks before his death. He wasn't as spry as he once was, but he showed up to fulfill the important mission God had given him during his eighty-six years on this earth. It's a blessing to live out the life purpose, meaning, and mission we were called to from eternity. And as crazy as the world may be, you can be assured that God has an exciting mission for you—no matter your age—up to the day He takes you home to heaven. So I ask you, "Will you maintain your life mission or rust out?"

FINISHING WELL

Before we wrap up this chapter, I want to note that we never reach an age that God cannot use us for His purpose and mission. Famous evangelist Billy Graham, at age ninety-four, wrote the following in his New York Times Best-Selling book, *Nearing Home: Life, Faith and Finishing Well*:

> *The Bible does not picture us in our latter years as useless and ineffective, condemned to spend our last days in endless boredom or meaningless activity until God finally takes us home.*[76]

In that deeply personal memoir, Dr. Graham reflects on his life, God's gifts, and the challenges of aging while maintaining his commitment to faith and finishing well. He shows us that even in our last years, we can still live out our purpose and mission until we leave this earth in bodily form. He also addresses finding purpose and encourages his readers to find God's purpose in their later years, suggesting that older people can still be useful and have a significant impact on others in this world. I am personally reminded of Psalm 138:8 which says, *The Lord will fulfill his purpose for me; your steadfast love, O Lord, endures forever. Do not forsake the work of your hands.*

That verse begs the question: Where are you in seeking true purpose in your life? To help you answer and define that question, I challenge you to ask God to help you answer five questions:

1) How can I lead a significant life?
2) To what specific areas have I been called in order to obtain personal meaning and purpose?
3) What mission have I been building and have been called to in effort to make a difference in the world?
4) Where are You leading me to impact the world?
5) In light of wanting to excel, am I willing to accept the mission in light of my life purpose?

At this point in our journey, we get to the final chapter of this book regarding mission with purpose. And that centers on what we leave behind—our legacy.

14

BUILD A LASTING LEGACY

Everyone leaves a legacy, whether they want to or not.
The question is, "What kind of legacy will you leave?"[77]
–Dillon Burroughs

Douglas Tompkins, co-founder of The North Face company and Tompkins Conservation, illustrates the power of legacy in that he sold his business to pursue a life of adventure and conservation. He and his wife, Kris, bought over two million acres of, primarily, Chilean and Argentine land, to protect it from development and to create new national parks. His legacy lives on not only in The North Face brand but also in the conservation and parks that thousands of people enjoy every year. And then there is Reverend Billy Graham (1918–2018). His legacy continues through BGEA (Billy Graham Evangelistic Association). During his lifetime, he preached to nearly 215 million people across 185 countries and in the process shaped modern evangelicalism. Known as "America's Pastor," he advised every U.S. president from Harry S. Truman to Donald J. Trump, bridging faith and politics.

Legacies represent the enduring impact that our actions, words, achievements, creations, and character leave behind for future generations. They live on in our children and relatives, other loved ones, those impacted by our work and ministry, and many more. Our legacy will influence generations long after we are gone. My father's death left my family with a legacy that in some ways was larger than life. He was a man of integrity, a great husband and father, a provider and leader. My father's legacy was one of non-wavering commitment to my mother, his children, hard work, and success. He loved God, America, Italy, and all things family. He worked hard, appreciating all that America had to offer that his birth country, Italy, and most other places around the world did not have at that time.

My father's legacy led to my mother's ability to raise their four children on her own. When she speaks of my father's legacy, she gives full credit to God's hand on her life and her children's for how our family developed. Under God, she kept our close-knit family together and driven to move ahead in our schooling, work ethic, respect, and love for one another and others.

But if you don't have a strong family legacy like mine, it's never too late to change that by building a legacy for yourself and your family. That said, let's make sure not to confuse legacy with success.

LEGACY AND SUCCESS

Success can reflect legacy, but it does not define it because legacy in great part is developed by what you do with your talents, gifts, and skills in light of God's plan for your life. If you have material and monetary success but don't pursue God's will, your legacy will be finite and temporal because it benefits you as opposed to others. Even if you make billions of dollars and give it all to your children—if you were not there to invest yourself in their lives, your legacy is limited to a temporal financial transaction. Buildings decay and fall apart. Cars grow old and rust out. Professional titles and accomplishments fade, and professional designations and positions end. Nobody will remember who you and I are 100 years from now.

However, your efforts and how you use your resources, opportunities, wealth, and time are never forgotten by God, whether good or bad. Going back to the law of identity, our legacy is carried into time through and by our name. Growing up, I was told never to bring disgrace upon the Garofalo name. King Solomon tells us, *A good name is better than precious ointment, and the day of death than the day of birth* (Ecclesiastes 7:1).

A GOOD NAME FROM ANCIENT TIMES

To gain some ancient, supernatural wisdom regarding a good name, let's break down King Solomon's counsel in Ecclesiastes 7:1. The two parts of this verse fit together like a puzzle in that *the day of death* is better if one has made *a good name* for himself so his life has a continuing influence. In other words, a person's death may be better than the day of his or her birth if their name, their legacy, leaves a lasting good reputation. Like ointment or perfume, which was desirable and expensive in Solomon's day, a good reputation and legacy is valuable. Solomon also tells us, *A good name is to be chosen rather than great riches, and favor is better than silver or gold* (Proverbs 22:1). Our legacy is of great value, but it's not secured in eternity until after our death. We should not become obsessed with death, though; rather, we should focus on living a godly life of purpose, meaning, and mission in the present. We should think about death and allow the past to instruct our future, because everyone leaves a legacy, and we are wise to leave a godly one.

Jesus confirmed that mission with purpose is the driver for a meaningful, purpose-filled life. The last commandment Jesus gave to (left for) His followers before ascending into heaven was "*Go therefore and make disciples of all nations*" (Matthew 28:19). This is a clear, specific mission driven by deep meaning and purpose. As a result, His disciples changed the world forever. The act of forging our legacy must be framed with purpose, meaning, and mission, which have no earthly termination point. At the end of chapter 14, I mentioned my mentor, Dr. Geisler. His legacy, in addition to starting two seminaries, was in his students not a physical building. For the nineteen years I knew Dr. Geisler, his mission in great part was to "train the trainer" and pass the baton to the next generation.

LETTING GO AND PASSING THE BATON

In great part, our legacy mandates that we release our power, wealth, and position by handing them to the next generation. These blessings should not be pried out of our dead hands. Letting go is simply giving up what is beyond our control to keep in the long run. In Isaiah 43:18–19, God said to His people through the prophet Isaiah, *"Remember not the former things, nor consider the things of old. Behold, I am doing a new thing; now it springs forth, do you not perceive it? I will make a way in the wilderness and rivers in the desert."*

The key phrase here is "*Behold, I [God] am doing a new thing*" (v.19). What makes us think that we should, or even could, change, hinder, or oppose God's new thing by failing to pass the baton—by clinging to the things of this world until we die? This is especially prevalent with people of power and influence, who more often than not have great difficulty releasing that power and position.

Consider certain members of the U.S. House of Representatives and the U.S. Senate. Many of these leaders grow old and die in office, failing to let go and let God; instead they cling to their power and position until their last breath. Examples include Senators John McCain and Diane Feinstein, who both died in office, failing to pass the torch to a more able, younger person who would be better able to lead. Neither politician was able to carry out the duties of their job and position. Feinstein was in a wheelchair, and her daughter had to communicate for her; John McCain had a brain tumor that impaired his ability to lead. Think of how their legacy might have been different had they passed the baton to a person they mentored before passing away as opposed to losing their ability to function while clinging to power.

Too many people think like the Egyptian pharaohs, assuming they will continue to rule into the afterlife instead of preparing others to take the baton of their role to carry on for the nation and the world. When people hold so tightly to the past that they miss the new things God has for them, they miss what God wants to show them in the present, at that stage in their life. God warns us that we cannot control the past, but we can focus on what He has for us in the present, despite how old we are. Failing to let go may not be easy, but we should opt for the betterment of others in light of our eternal purpose as opposed to our earthly desires. An example of this being done rightly is illustrated in Coca-Cola Consolidated Chairman and CEO J. Frank Harrison III, who provides us with some practical ways to build and leave a strong legacy.

FORMULA FOR A LASTING LEGACY

Harrison says that we are wise to build our legacy proactively and not reactively. In *The Transformation Factor: Leading Your Company for Good, for God, and for Growth,* he outlines how we can do this:

> *Your legacy begins now. Though legacy is an accumulation of life and work, a lasting legacy is the sum of not only what you do but also who you are. What I mean by that is the type of person you are, the virtues you possess, and the character you cultivate. Transformational leaders begin with a legacy mindset. They must not fall into the trap of barreling through life and work, hoping that their achievements will amount to something. I've seen too many leaders take that approach and then have to deal with the problems it produces. Instead, leading with the end in mind forces you to consider the reason why you do things or make certain decisions."* [78]

Harrison's formula regarding legacy is an excellent blueprint for building our own legacy. Let's take a more in-depth look at a couple of key takeaways Harrison provides. The secret formula for making Coca-Cola is secured in a vault, but J. Frank Harrison was kind enough to share his formula for leaving a good legacy. I highly recommend getting the book and reading it for yourself. Let's take a look.

First, Harrison writes that your legacy begins by taking action *now.* We tend to procrastinate what should and can be done today. Jesus said, "*We must work the works of him who sent me while it is day; the night is coming, when no one can work*" (John 9:4). Procrastination is the enemy of success and growth. We are all terminal, and we all leave a legacy. Why not leave a good one instead of a bad one? James, the brother of Jesus wrote, *Yet you do not know what tomorrow will bring. What is your life? For you are a mist that appears for a little time and then vanishes* (James 4:14).

Second, Harrison points out that a strong legacy will last through generations yet to come. He says that although legacy is an accumulation of life and work, a lasting legacy is the sum of not only what you do but also who you are (your character): the type of person you are, the virtues you possess, and the character you cultivate. In other words, you and I are guaranteed to leave a legacy. The question is, what will that legacy be?

Harrison closes out his book with the following words:

> *I really got into the word "legacy" after James [his son] died. I'd really not thought much about it before. It's a power concept. As we discussed earlier, it's not like inheritance, where you leave money and resources, assets, and land to people. Rather, legacy is about what you leave in people that goes on and on. Legacy is what people say about you after you're gone. Which, of course, makes a real legacy an eternal one. The only way I've been able to figure that one out is through a relationship with Christ and his promise of eternal life. …*[80]
>
> *Don't waste your life. Don't withdraw. Stay in the game. … I want to encourage you, regardless of the circumstances, to continue to fight the good fight and press on! The Great Commission is alive and well. It doesn't say that when you make a lot of money and move to the retirement home in the mountains that you don't have to worry about the Great Commission anymore. No! God wants us to finish life strong for him. We need to move now while our day is here. Whatever you are going to do for Jesus, you better do now.*[81]

A CONTINUING INFLUENCE

If Harrison can do it, so can you and I. Many leaders who have achieved wealth, fame, and power find it more difficult to give of themselves selflessly. Mr. Harrison and his family are very generous, godly-mission people. I challenge you to write down what you can do with the opportunities, talents, gifts, and skills God has given you in light of defining your legacy. Remember, all things in this world are material and temporal unless used rightly in forging your own legacy.

In life, purpose-driven missions come in numerous forms. We wake each morning to a new day, which offers and sometimes mandates that we act without delay. That action is driven by a purpose we have been called to for a particular moment, and accomplishing the mission gives us meaning for that day. Going back to the 1988 earthquake story in chapter one, Armon's father did not go to bed thinking that his mission and purpose the next morning would be to keep his word and save his son and other children. He didn't ask for that mission—it was a by-product of natural evil that necessitated his good action. Had Armon's father not accepted his purpose for that day and the seemingly hopeless mission at hand, his son along with thirteen other children would have died.

There are also long-term life purpose(s) such as maintaining a strong marriage, raising children, building a career, and helping others prosper. These goals all have purpose and meaning that we work out in the larger realm of our overall life mission. In either case, meaning and mission start with purpose.

Throughout this book I've used examples of people who lived out their mission with either sinful or godly purposes. Yes, there are tyrants and murderers who have abused and exploited people for personal gain. But there are also individuals such as Billy Graham, Mother Theresa, and many others who have helped millions of people in a positive way. Some in the marketplace, like the leadership at Coca-Cola Consolidated, fulfill their purpose through sound business practices and charitable acts, such as assisting people and communities during natural disasters and other difficult circumstances.

But what about you and me? Most of us reading this book aren't famous, don't own corporations, and don't serve in full-time nonprofit work. Still, I hope that what you've read in this book has convinced you that God has given you a unique purpose-filled mission which will provide deep meaning and a lasting legacy. Remember, Armon's father was not famous or professionally qualified for search-or-rescue. He wasn't even asked to take on his daily mission. Quite the opposite. He was told to abandon it. Yet part of his legacy includes his son and the thirteen other children he saved that day and the impact they and their families had on others.

Let's remember the words of King Solomon who wisely tells us, *For the living know that they will die, but the dead known nothing, and they have no more reward, for the memory of them is forgotten*" (Ecclesiastes 9:5). What is not forgotten is the legacy we leave (good or bad). Our efforts and how we use our resources, opportunities, wealth, and time are carried into the next generation and into eternity. If we have made a *good name* (our legacy), which is forged in our lifetime, our life will have a continuing influence for good and for God. Everyone lives their life with some kind of purpose and mission. And as a result, everyone leaves a legacy. What will be yours?

ENDNOTES

1. "Aloo Denish Obiero | Quotes| Quotable Quotes," Goodreads, https://www.goodreads.com/quotes/11911060-vision-sees-the-stars-mission-carves-the-path-to-reach.

2. Billy Graham, *Hope for the Troubled Heart* (Dallas: Word, 1991), ix.

3. Viktor E. Frankl | Quotes | Quotable Quotes" Goodreads, https://www.go-odreads com/quotes/10747274-if-you-don-t-know-what-your-mission-in-life-is.

4. Jordan Raynor, *The Sacredness of Secular Work: 4 Ways Your Job Matters for Eternity* (Even if You're Not Sharing the Gospel (Colorado Springs, CO: WaterBrook-Penguin Random House), 2024, 13.

5. "A Father's Love," Crossway, accessed March 30, 2026, https://www.crossway.org/tracts/a-fathers-love-2770/.

6. John MacGregor, *The Top 10 Reasons the Rich God Broke: Powerful Stories That Will Transform Your Financial Life...Forever, Introduction* (Scottsdale, AZ: Eleuthera Press, an imprint of RDA Press, LLC.), 2020.

7. J. Frank Harrison III, *The Transformation Factor: Leading Your Company for Good, for God, and for Growth, First Edition* (Austin, TX: Greenleaf Book Group Press, 2022), 30.

8. J. Frank Harrison III, *The Transformation Factor*, 31–32.

9. *Welcome from Frank Harrison Coca-Cola Consolidated*, Vimeo, Religious Freedom & Business Foundation, August 20, 2022, https://vimeo.com/741356636.

10. Billy Graham, *Billy Graham in Quotes Library Selection*, Franklin Graham with Donna Lee Toney (Nashville, TN: Thomas Nelson 2011), 330.

11. "Jordan Raynor | Quotes" Goodreads, from Redeeming Your Time: *7 Biblical Principles for Being Purposeful, Present, and Wildly Productive*, https://www.goodreads.com/author/quotes/8300302.Jordan_Raynor.

12. T. D. Wilson, D. A. Reinhard, E. C. Westgate, D.T Gilbert, et al. "Just Think: The Challenges of the Disengaged Mind," Science 345, 75–77. 10.1126/science.1250830 (Sited by Boredom–understanding the emotion and its impact on our lives: an African perspective - PMC.

13. Dr. Yuhong Dong, "Purposeful People Live Longer—and Better, According to Research," *The Epoch Times*, TheEpochTimes.com, December 25, 2022, https://www.theepochtimes.com/health/purposeful-people-live-longer-and-better-according-to-research_4924181.html?utm_source=Bright&src_src=Bright&utm_campaign=bright-2022-12-26&src_cmp=bright-2022-12-26&utm_medium=email&est=p6wPhPbriJCLuUOVl9Mceui5Xj3%2BG3%2BqcaG4jAurwbd27KjEv4LfpR9WNpMD.

14. Dr. Yuhong Dong, "Purposeful People Live Longer."

15. Rick Warren, *The Purpose Driven Life: What On Earth Am I Hear For?* (Grand Rapids, MI: Zondervan, 2002), 17.

16. Andrew: Inside & Insights, "Vision and Purpose in the Marketplace," Andrew Ong, July 16, 2009, https://andrew-ong.com/2009/07/16/vision-and-purpose-in-the-marketplace/.

17. Bill Gates, *Bartlett's Familiar Quotations*, John Bartlett, Geoffrey O'Brien, General Editors, (NY: Little, Brown and Company Inc. 2012), 873.

18. The Westminster Standard, *Shorter Catechism Text and Scripture Proofs*, https://thewestminsterstandard.org/westminster-shorter-catechism/.

19. Billy Graham, *Hope for the Troubled Heart* (Dallas: Word, 1991), 104.

20. C. S. Lewis, *The Problem of Pain* (NY: HarperCollins, 2001), 88–89. (See *Reflections*, February 2009, *Surrender*.)

21. Rosie Frost, Euro News, "Living in a Bubble: Did This Failed 90s Experiment Predict the Future?" January 29, 2022, https://www.euronews.com/green/2022/01/29/living-in-a-bubble-did-this-failed-90s-experiment-predict-the-future.

22. *Biosphere2*, University of Arizona, https://biosphere2.org/.

23. Viktor E. Frankl, *Man's Search for Meaning* (Boston: Beacon Press, 2017), 70.

24. Viktor E. Frankl, *Man's Search for Meaning*, 70.

25. Hu Shi, "Our Attitude Toward Modern Western Civilization," (Columbia University, Asia for Educators) https://afe.easia.columbia.edu/ps/cup/hushi_western_civ.pdf.

26. "John D. Rockefeller," *New World Encyclopedia*, 9 https://www.newworldencyclopedia.org/entry/John_D._Rockefeller.

27. "John D. Rockefeller | In an Interview 1905," John Bartlett, Geoffrey O'Brien, general editor, Bartlett's Familiar Quotations, Eighteenth Edition (NY: Little, Brown and Company, 2012), 535.

28. "John D. Rockefeller," *New World Encyclopedia*, 9.

29. Allison Millington, "The Founder of Lululemon Is Now One of the 500 Richest People in the World," *Business Insider*, BusinessInsider.com, September 6, 2018 6:01 AM EDT , https://link.edgepilot.com/s/9ffe8b68/4r7IYfBdqESFh-lb5AR7NQ?u=https://www.businessinsider.com/lululemon-founder-chip-wilson-richest-people-2018-9.

30. Jeremiah Burroughs, "The Power of Christian Contentment: Finding Deeper, Richer, Christ-centered Joy" by Andrew M. Davis, sourced from Jeremy Burroughs, *The Rare Jewel of Christian Contentment* (Carlisle, PA: Banner of Truth, 2013), 19.

31. Patrick M. Morley, *The Man in the Mirror: Solving the 24 Problems Men Face*, 25th Anniversary Edition (Grand Rapids, MI: Zondervan Books, 2014),106.

32. Morley, *The Man in the Mirror*, 107.

33. Morley, *The Man in the Mirror*, 107–108.

34. Roy B. Zuck, *The Speakers Quote Book* (Grand Rapids, MI: Kregel Books, 1997), 87.

35. Zuck, *The Speakers Quote Book*, 260.

36. Moses Maimonides, Originally published ca 1190, *The Guide for the Perplexed; Bartlett's Familiar Quotations*, John Bartlett, (NY: Little, Brown and Company Inc., 2012), 124.

37. "Identity-Self-Image, Self Concept," Psychology Today, https://www.psychology-today.com/us/basics/identity#:~:text=What%20defines%20identity?,Created%20with%20Sketch.

38. Cole A. Randall, "My Favorite Quotes on Success, Significance, and Failure," Medium, https://medium.com/@cole_53948/my-favorite-quotes-on-success-significance-and-failure-852c4d41e9bd.

39. Tony Robbins, "*Discover the 6 Human Needs*," Tony Robins Blog, https://www.tonyrobbins.com/blog/do-you-need-to-feel-significant?srsltid=AfmBOooTh-qnA2dxXdJx7tWUKG3WX6RAJVWK1FrsJLHFjvpfrCPvUZtVC.

40. "Friedrich Nietzsche |Quotes |Quotable Quotes," Goodreads, Quote by Friedrich Nietzsche: "He who has a why to live for can bear almost an ..."

41. Viktor E. Frankl, *What Is Logotherapy?*, Victor Frankl America/VFIA, https://viktorfranklamerica.com/what-is-logotherapy/.

42. Coca-Cola Consolidated, "Our Purpose," https://www.cokeconsolidated.com/about-us/

43. Rick Warren, *The Purpose Driven Life: What on Earth Am I Here For?* (Grand Rapids, MI: Zondervan Publishers, 2002), 17.

44. Derwin L. Gray, *Limitless Life: You Are More Than Your Past When God Holds Your Future*, (Thomas Nelson Publishers, Nashville, TN, 2013), 157.

45. Martin Buber, John Bartlett, Geoffrey O'Brien, general editors, B*artlett's Familiar Quotations* (NY: Little, Brown and Company Inc., 2012), 634.

46. Laura Carrione, "Hobby Lobby Founder Explains Decision to 'Give Away Ownership' of Company: 'Joy in Giving What We Have'", Business Leaders, November 14, 2022 1:21 pm EST, https://www.foxbusiness.com/retail/hobby-lobby-founder-explains-decision-give-away-ownership-company-joy-giving.

47. Peterson, *12 Rules for Life*, (Toronto: Canada, Random House Canada, a division of Penguin Random House Canada Ltd., 2018), 201.

48. Simon Jacobson, *Toward a Meaningful Life: The Wisdom of Rebbe Menachem Mendel Schneerson*, (NY: HarperCollins Publishers, 2019), 144–145.

ENDNOTES

49. Peterson, *12 Rules for Life*, 201.

50. *The Billy Graham Christian Worker's Handbook* (Charlotte, NC: BGEA, 1984), 88.

51. John Coleman, "Finding Success Starts with Finding Your Purpose," Harvard Business Review, January 11, 2022, https://hbr.org/2022/01/finding-success-starts-with-finding-your-purpose.

52. Bobby Owsinksi, "*87.6% of All Musicians Releasing Music Are 'Undiscovered*'," HYPEBOT, 03/15/2024. https://www.hypebot.com/hypebot/2024/02/87-6-of-all-musicians-releasing-music-are-undiscovered.html#:~:text=A%20new%20Chartmetric%20report%20puts,establish%20a%20brand%20or%20following.

53. Katarina Ahlin, "Luck and Timing: Crucial for Success?" CFR Global Executive Search, https://www.cfr-group.com/luck-and-timing-crucial-for-success/.

54. Peter Ho, "Why Does Chance Play a Major Role When It Comes to Success in Life?" Quora, https://www.quora.com/Why-does-chance-play-a-major-role-when-it-comes-to-success-in-life.

55. *The Billy Graham Christian Worker's Handbook*, 88.

56. John Coleman, "Finding Success Starts with Finding Your Purpose."

57. Viktor E. Frankl, *Man's Search for Meaning*, xvii.

58. Jordon Peterson, "Bearing Responsibility Might Be the Key to Happiness, Personality," Brian Kilmeade interview, Fox News, August 19, 2023, https://www.foxnews.com/video/6334706836112.

59. Eugene Adu-Wusu, "The Meaning of Success and How to Define Success in Life," Linkedin, February 3, 2016, https://www.linkedin.com/pulse/meaning-success-how-define-life-eugene-adu-wusu/.

60. Eugene Adu-Wusu, "The Meaning of Success."

61. Steve Diggs, *Free to Succeed: 12 Dynamic Keys to Experiencing and Enjoying Godly Success* (Tarrytown, NY: Fleming H. Revell Company, 1992), 38.

62. Steve Diggs, *Free to Succeed*, 38–44.

63. Viktor E. Frankl, *Man's Search for Meaning*, xvii.

64. "Soren Kierkegaard | Quotes," https://www.goodreads.com/quotes/328259-what-i-really-lack-is-to-be-clear-in-my.

65. "William Carey | How William Carey Expected Great Things From God, Calvarychapel.Com," Jasmine Alnutt, https://calvarychapel.com/posts/how-william-carey-expected-great-things-from-god/.

66. Albert Einstein, *The Speaker's Quote Book* (Grand Rapids, MI: Kregel Publications, 1997), 347.

67. Franklin Graham with Donna Lee Toney, *Billy Graham in Quotes* (Dallas, TX: Thomas Nelson, 2011), 139.

68. Franklin Graham with Donna Lee Toney, Billy Graham in Quotes (Dallas, TX: Thomas Nelson, 2011), 139.

69. John MacArthur, "Why God Pulls You Away from People After 50," Refined Strength Podcast, https://youtu.be/KDneI_qUOCU?si=RLZNWeXpaQpB3dSZ.

70. Nellah Baily Mc Gough, "90 Retirement Quotes That Will Resonate with Any Retiree," *Southern Living*, September 25, 2025, https://share.google/dyXyjbrgM-DwC9hbhO.

71. Pete Honiotes, CFP, "What You Might Regret About Early Retirement—and How to Avoid It," CreativePlanning.Com, September 11, 2024, https://creative-planning.com/insights/retirement/reasons-not-retire-early/.

72. Samantha Gibson, "The Pros and Cons of Early Retirement," Canaccord Wealth, July 10, 2025, https://www.google.com/search?q=the+pros+of+retirement&sca_es-v=37da6120ca4cbbd6&rlz=1C1CHBF_enUS1174US1174&ei=jd5WabHhFfKF-wbkPt4u0yAc&ved=0ahUKEwjx24GrnOuRAxXyQjA.

73. Aaron Renn Blog, "The Retreat of the Successful: Why Local Businesses Are Disappearing-and So Are the People Who Once Built Them," Guest writer Justin Powell, April 1, 2025, https://www.aaronrenn.com/p/the-retreat-of-the-successful.

74. Dr. Yuhon Dong, "Purposeful People Live Longer—and Better—According to Research," TheEpochTimes.Com, Published December 25, 2022, https://www.theepochtimes.com/health/purposeful-people-live-longer-and-better-according-to-research_4924181.html?utm_source=Bright&src_src=Bright&utm_campaign=bright-2022-12-26&src_cmp=bright-2022-12-26&utm_medium=email&est=p6wPhPbriJCLuUOVl9Mceui5Xj3%2BG3%2BqcaG4jAurwbd27KjE-v4LfpR9WNpMD.

75. Breakwater Financial, LLC, "A Brief History of Retirement," May 17, 2019, http://breakwaterfinancial.com/blog/a-brief-history-of-retirement#:~:text=During%20the%201950's%20we%20start,period%20of%20retirement%20in%20America.

76. Billy Graham, *Nearing Home—Life, Faith and Finishing Well* (Nashville, TN: Thomas Nelson Publishers, 2013), vii.

77. "Dillon Burroughs | Quotes | Quotable Quotes," Goodreads, *Quote by Dillon Burroughs: "Everyone leaves a legacy, whether they want to ..."*

78. J. Frank Harrison III, *The Transformation Factor: Leading Your Company for Good, for God, and for Growth*, First edition, (Austin, TX: Greenleaf Book Group Press, 2022), 14.

79. J. Frank Harrison III, *The Transformation Factor*, 14.

80. J. Frank Harrison III, *The Transformation Factor*, 145–146.

81. J. Frank Harrison III, *The Transformation Factor*, 146–147.

82. Billy Graham, *The Journey* (Nashville: W Publishing Group, 2006), 73.

83. *Steps to Peace with God* witnessing tract, Crossway.org, published 2006, Good News Publishers and Crossway Books.

APPENDIX

HOW DO I KNOW THAT I AM GOING TO HEAVEN?

"Your salvation depends on what [Christ] has done for you, not on what you do for Him. It isn't your hold on God that saves you; it's His hold on you."
— Billy Graham[82]

CAN I REALLY KNOW THAT I AM GOING TO HEAVEN?

Yes, absolutely. We can be sure about where we will spend eternity when we pass from this earth and leave our earthen body. We can know with certainty that when we die, we will go to heaven. How can we be sure? This is a question that many people have struggled with, especially folks who are seeking God or who are new believers in Jesus Christ.

The Bible outlines how to have peace with God—it comes only through Jesus Christ. Most people have an idea of what they believe it will take to be accepted by God. After all, who likes the idea of exiting this life without being on good terms with him? Thankfully, it's possible to be certain that you've made peace with God, but the way must be chosen during this life. Here are the steps drawn from God's book the Bible laid out by the Billy Graham Evangelistic Association.

STEPS TO PEACE WITH GOD:

The Bible teaches that the assurance of salvation rests securely upon four unshakable pillars:

STEP 1. UNDERSTAND GOD'S PURPOSES—PEACE AND ETERNAL LIFE

God loves you and wants you to experience peace and an eternal, fulfilling life.

The Bible says…

"We have peace with God through our Lord Jesus Christ." Romans 5:1

"For God so loved the world, that he gave his only Son, that whoever believes in him should not perish but have eternal life." John 3:16

"I came that they may have life and have it abundantly." John 10:10

Why don't most people have this peace and the fulfilling (abundant) life that God intended for us to have?

STEP 2. ADMIT THE PROBLEM—OUR SIN AND SEPARATION

God did not create us like robots to automatically love and mechanically obey him. God gave us a will and the freedom to choose. The first man and woman chose to disobey God and go their own willful way. And we still make that choice today. This results in separation from God.

The Bible says...

"For all have sinned and fall short of the glory of God." Romans 3:23

"For the wages of sin is death." Romans 6:23

People have tried many ways to bridge this gap between themselves and God.

The Bible says ...

"There is a way that seems right to a man, but its end is the way to death." Proverbs 14:12

"Your iniquities have made a separation between you and your God ..." Isaiah 59:2

No bridge reaches God ... except one.

STEP 3. DISCOVER GOD'S BRIDGE—THE CROSS

Jesus Christ died on the cross and rose from the grave. Though he was

God's sinless Son, he became a human, took our place, and paid the penalty for our sin, bridging the gap between God and us.

The Bible says...

> *"For there is one God, and there is one mediator between God and men, the man Christ Jesus."* 1 Timothy 2:5

> *"Christ ... suffered once for sins, the righteous for the unrighteous, that he might bring us to God."* 1 Peter 3:18

> *"God shows his love for us in that while we were still sinners, Christ died for us ... the free gift of God is eternal life in Christ Jesus our Lord."* Romans 5:8, 3:23

> *"Christ died for our sins ... he was buried ... he was raised on the third day."* 1 Corinthians 15:3-4

God has provided the only way to forgiveness of sin and eternal life. But each person must make a choice.

STEP 4. EMBRACE THE TRUTH—RECEIVE CHRIST

We must trust Jesus Christ as our Savior and receive him by personal choice.

Jesus says...

> *"Behold, I stand at the door and knock. If anyone hears my voice and opens the door, I will come in and eat with him, and he with me."* Revelation 3:20

"I am the way, and the truth, and the life. No one comes to the Father except through me." John 14:6

The Bible says...

"To all who did receive him, who believed in his name, he gave the right to become children of God." John 1:12

"Whoever believes in the Son has eternal life." John 3:36

WHAT IS YOUR DECISION?

Will you receive Jesus Christ right now and trust in him alone for forgiveness and eternal life? The Bible says that's the only way to find peace with God!

- Admit your need—that you are a sinner in need of God's forgiveness.
- Be willing to turn from trusting in anything else for eternal life and trust only in Christ.
- Believe that Jesus Christ died for you on the cross, came back to life from the grave, and is your only way to heaven.
- Accept Jesus' offer to forgive your sins and come into your life as your Savior.

You may want to tell him in words like these:

"Dear Jesus, thank you for making it possible for me to find peace with God! I believe that when you died you were paying the penalty for my sins. I now receive you into my life as my Savior, so I can have forgiveness and never-ending life from God! Thank you for the gift of eternal life!" [83]

BEYOND THE PAGES

CONNECT WITH STEVEN GAROFALO

To connect with Steven Garofalo, having him speak at your organization, and for additional resources, scan the QR Code below.

www.ingramcontent.com/pod-product-compliance
Lightning Source LLC
LaVergne TN
LVHW010923110826
845149LV00013B/2464

* 9 7 8 0 9 8 9 7 4 4 6 8 3 *